ECONOMIC ISSUES, PROBLEMS AND PERSPECTIVES

LAFFER-KEYNESIAN SYNTHESIS AND MACROECONOMIC EQUILIBRIUM

ECONOMIC ISSUES, PROBLEMS AND PERSPECTIVES

Additional books in this series can be found on Nova's website under the Series tab.

Additional e-books in this series can be found on Nova's website under the e-book tab.

ECONOMIC ISSUES, PROBLEMS AND PERSPECTIVES

LAFFER-KEYNESIAN SYNTHESIS AND MACROECONOMIC EQUILIBRIUM

IURI ANANIASHVILI
AND
VLADIMER PAPAVA

NOVINKA

New York

For permission to use material from this book please contact us:
Telephone 631-231-7269; Fax 631-231-8175
Web Site: http://www.novapublishers.com

LIBRARY OF CONGRESS CATALOGING-IN-PUBLICATION DATA

Laffer-keynesian Synthesis and Macroeconomic Equilibrium / Iuri Ananiashvili and Vladimer Papava
p. cm.
Includes index.
ISBN 978-1-62948-668-0 (Softcover)
1. Laffer-keynesian Synthesis and Macroeconomic Equilibrium
TP1180.S7P75 2010
668.4'233--dc22
2010047082

Published by Nova Science Publishers, Inc. † New York

CONTENTS

PREFACE

One of the most urgent topics of economics and economic policy is the impact of tax burden on the economic activity of the population at large and on the mobilization of tax revenues in a national budget. At present, the interest of academic economists in this issue has been clearly increased (for example, Sowell, 2012).

The circumstance that without taxes no state and society can exist does not require any in-depth justification. At the same time, it is a widespread opinion among economists that taxes distort economic activities and decrease the efficiency of the market mechanism which leads to "unrecoverable losses" (for example, Mankiw, 2004, ch. 8; Sachs, & Larrain, 1993, ch. 7; Stiglitz, 1988, ch. 18-20) which refers to the potential effect that can be achieved by firms and households but which have not been achieved because the existing taxes make certain adjustments to the pattern of working and taking leave; consuming and investing, etc.

Such a double nature of taxes requires examination of their role at the macro level; i.e., it needs to be determined to what extent the tax regime and the tax rates affect the macroeconomic equilibrium and the employment level or, what is more essential: the overall positive effect secured by the government to the country's economy or the total losses due to the taxes. What is the optimal tax rate at which a maximum economic activity or maximum budget revenues, etc., are achieved?

In the recent period, the interest in the above issue and many other issues related to taxes has become even more apparent. A large number of publications contain justification or rejection of the Arthur Laffer Curve concept and explore issues of its practical realization. The present monograph resonates to the Laffer concept to some extent. At the same time, it puts an emphasis on identifying the role the average tax rate has on reaching the macroeconomic equilibrium.

It is known that reducing the average tax rate stimulates the aggregate supply in supply-side economics while it boosts the aggregate demand in the Keynesian model. Based on this causal relationship, the present study is the first more or less comprehensive monograph which examines the Laffer-Keynesian synthesis.

The authors will gladly take relevant suggestions from readers into consideration.

INTRODUCTION

The problem of achieving and maintaining stable economic growth has worsened in developed and developing countries during the global financial and economic crisis. This problem is no less important for transition economies. In this situation, it is natural that the problem of stable economic growth is one of the most topical issues for modern economics.

Many considerations are involved in examining the regularities regarding how changes (a decrease or increase) in the tax burden affect national budget revenues, on the one hand, and how these changes influence economic activities, on the other hand, and, consequently, how they affect employment and output rates. It is equally important to examine how government spending influences economic growth.

The Keynesian model of aggregate demand gives a quite comprehensive picture of how the tax burden influences economic growth. Though this model has been the subject of many studies and is well explored, it can be said that its analytical capabilities have not yet been fully examined. For instance, based on the study of key characteristics of one of the modified versions of the above-mentioned model, it has been established that the impact of the tax burden on aggregate demand cannot be determined unequivocally. Usually, an increase in the tax burden is one means of decreasing aggregate demand, but, at the same time, an increase in the tax burden may trigger an increase in aggregate demand under certain conditions.

The Laffer Curve is the most evident illustration of the key postulations of the supply-side economics. Presently, many economists are evidently critical of the Laffer Curve. Despite this, there is a number of most recent works aimed at studying mathematical and empirical implications of the Laffer Curve.

It is notable that the tax burden affects both the effectiveness of using productive resources, that is, production technology, and the level of resource usage. Both of these aspects of the tax burden are important, but the impact on the level of resource usage is especially important. The Laffer Effect refers to the result of this impact and it should be taken into consideration when working out a fiscal policy that boosts economic growth.

In order to achieve stable economic growth, it is extremely important to establish levels of the tax burden and government spending that will ensure optimization of the level of resource usage.

Keynesian models deal with the situation when aggregate supply is not dependent on tax rates, while aggregate demand, especially the part of it that relates to consumption, is the function of taxes. Supply-side economics also considers only a single aspect of the tax issue in the Laffer Curve, which emphasizes the impact of the tax rate on aggregate supply.[1] The single-sidedness of the above theories can be overcome by the Laffer-Keynesian synthesis (Papava, 1996, pp. 263-267; 1999, pp. 285-289; 2003, pp. 66-68). The model of macroeconomic equilibrium allows for this synthesis, in which aggregate demand and aggregate supply are represented as functions of the tax burden (Ananiashvili, & Papava, 2012a).[2] The appropriateness of such an approach for assessing the role of the tax burden in economics is also indicated by the fact that Arthur Laffer considered the idea of the Laffer Curve to belong not to himself but to John Maynard Keynes (Laffer, 2004).

[1] The different macroeconomic models "Keynesian/Traditional" and "Supply-Side/New Classical" are discussed in (Langdana, 2010, pp. 175-243).

[2] The results of Georgian economists were recognized internationally (for example, Balatsky, & Ekimova, 2012, pp. 63-64).

Chapter 1

AVERAGE TAX RATE AND THE KEYNESIAN MODEL OF AGGREGATE DEMAND

Since the 1930s, after John Maynard Keynes proposed the concept of government regulation of the economy, economists' interest in taxes has grown considerably. As we know, in this concept, taxes, along with government purchases and transfer payments, are supposed to play a significant role in regulating aggregate demand and, through aggregate demand, in solving problems of employment, inflation, and economic growth.[1]

In contemporary macroeconomics textbooks, the interrelation of taxes and aggregate demand is unambiguously defined: it is thought that increasing taxes has a negative effect on aggregate demand and that lowering them has a positive effect, since the main element of aggregate spending—the amount of household consumer spending—decreases in the former case and increases in the latter (for example, Blanchard, 2009, ch. 5; Dornbusch, & Fischer, 1990, ch. 3; Mankiw, 1992, ch. 9; Sachs, & Larrain, 1993, ch. 12). However, because every phenomenon, including a change in taxes, has two sides—positive and negative—by considering the relationship between taxes and aggregate demand only in this context, we significantly simplify the existing reality. It can be shown that, in a certain situation, a tax increase causes an increase in

[1] In contemporary economics, the role of fiscal policy and the tax system in not limited to their effect on aggregate demand. A new doctrine emerged in the 1970s (supply-side economics), in which taxes and the tax system came to be seen as a purely fiscal tool that the government can use to stimulate business activity not through aggregate demand, but through reduction of the tax burden. However, this aspect of taxes is not addressed in this Chapter (it will be discussed in the following Chapter 2). For more details about the role of taxes and tax policy in government regulation of the economy, see, for example, (Atkinson, & Stiglitz, 1980; Stiglitz, 1988).

aggregate demand and a tax cut causes a decrease (Ananiashvili, 2008). We will consider this question in greater detail.

1.1. First Version of the Keynesian Model

The explanation of the mechanism and pattern of the average tax rate's influence on aggregate demand is traditionally based on using a modeling method. We will turn to this method and first consider the simplest standard Keynesian model of equilibrium in the market for goods and services, which can be written as follows (for example, Blanchard, 2009, ch. 6; Dornbusch, & Fischer, 1990, ch. 3; Mankiw, 1992, ch. 9; Sachs, & Larrain, 1993, ch. 12):

$$E = C + I + G + NX, \tag{1.1}$$

$$C = a + b(Y - T), \tag{1.2}$$

$$I = I_0, \quad G = G_0, \quad NX = NX_0 \tag{1.3}$$

$$T = T(Y), \tag{1.4}$$

$$Y = E, \tag{1.5}$$

where E is aggregate spending; C is household consumption; I is gross domestic private investments; G is government purchases; NX is net exports; a is autonomous consumption; b is marginal propensity of households to consume, $0 < b < 1$; T is net taxes (the difference between taxes and transfers); and Y is gross domestic product (GDP).

In this system, conditions (1.1)–(1.4) determine aggregate spending. According to (1.2), the element C of this spending is a linear function of current disposable income $(Y - T)$. As for the remaining three elements, I, G, and NX, for the sake of simplicity it is understood that they are given exogenously in the model and fixed at the levels I_0, G_0, and NX_0, respectively, as indicated in (1.3).

The condition corresponding to net taxes (1.4) requires special scrutiny. Traditionally, in a simple model such as (1.1)–(1.5) it is either accepted that taxes are of a lump-sum nature,[2] and $T = T_0$, where is a fixed amount, or a linear taxation system is considered, in which is defined as a linear function of Y. In the laverage Tax Rateer case, depending on what form of taxation $T(Y)$ describes, three possible versions can be considered: functions corresponding to proportional, linearly progressive, and linearly regressive taxation (for example, Atkinson, & Stiglitz, 1980, ch. 2).

In the case of proportional taxation,

$$T(Y) = t_1 Y - t_2 t_1 Y = (1 - t_2) t_1 Y = tY \,, \tag{1.6}$$

where, t_1 is the marginal tax rate, which, at the same time, coincides with the average tax rate; t_2 is the average rate of transfers and subsidies; and $t = (1 - t_2)t_1$ is the average rate of net taxation.

With linearly progressive taxation,

$$T(Y) = t_1 Y - T_R \,,$$

where is a given fixed amount of transfers and subsidies $(T_R > 0)$.

It is obvious that this function corresponds to a value of the average net taxation rate that increases in relation to $Y : t = T / Y$.

With linearly regressive taxation,[3]

$$T(Y) = (\widetilde{T} + t_1 Y) - t_2(\widetilde{T} + t_1 Y) = (1 - t_2)(\widetilde{T} + t_1 Y) \,,$$

where is the amount of tax that does not depend on income.

We should point out that in model (1.1)–(1.5), the consideration of any of the functions given here in the role of makes it possible to draw almost the

---

[2] A lump-sum, or fixed, tax is one whose amount does not depend on the tax base.

[3] The concepts of progressive and regressive taxation are defined in various ways in the economic literature. The approach used in our case is the one that Atkinson and Stiglitz rely on (Atkinson, & Stiglitz, 1980, ch. 2). Taxation is progressive when the average tax rate rises with income growth. In the case of regressive taxation, the average tax rate decreases with an increase in income.

same conclusions. Therefore, we will dwell on just one of them, for example, (1.6).

Henceforth we will call the system (1.1)–(1.6) *First Version of the Keynesian Model.*

Taking into account conditions (1.2), (1.3), and (1.6), in (1.1) we get:

$$E = b(1-t)Y + I_0 + G_0 + NX_0 + a.$$

With a fixed level of prices (which takes place in the model under consideration), *E*, which is determined by the given equation, can be regarded as the value of aggregate demand. As we see, *E* depends on the aggregated average tax rate *t* and, all else being equal, decreases in relation to the latter. In turn, in model (1.1)–(1.6), for a given fixed level of prices, the output (supply) of GDP amounts to *Y*. This implies that it is completely determined by aggregate demand.

In such conditions, the value of equilibrium GDP is determined from the equilibrium equation of the market for products and services (1.5):

$$Y = \lambda_1 A_1, \tag{1.7}$$

where is the amount of autonomous spending:

$$A_1 = a + I_0 + G_0 + NX_0, \tag{1.8}$$

and is autonomous spending multiplier:

$$\lambda_1 = \frac{1}{1-b(1-t)}. \tag{1.9}$$

Since the multiplier λ_1 decreases in relation to t (1.7)–(1.9) formally lead to the following conclusions:

1. For given autonomous spending (all else being equal), equilibrium output is a decreasing function of t. At the same time, if we assume that can take extreme values from 0 to 1, then the equilibrium output is maximum when and minimum when t = 1. In particular,

$Y_{max} = A_1/(1-b)$, $Y_{min} = A_1$.

2. For given autonomous spending, the net budget revenues (net taxes T) corresponding to equilibrium output are an increasing function of t. T is maximum when and minimum when $t = 0$. In this case,

$T_{max} = A_1$, and $T_{min} = 0$.

3. For given , the equilibrium output and corresponding budget revenues increase (or decrease) when there is an increase (or decrease) in autonomous spending A_1, of which one of the elements is government purchases G_0.

The curves in Figure 1.1 show that, all else being equal, in the standard Keynesian model, with a change in the average tax rate the values of equilibrium output and the corresponding net budget revenues change. Here we should point out that a change, an increase, for example, in causes simultaneous upward movement of the curves corresponding to and Y.

With aggregate supply that does not depend on , which takes place in model (1.1)–(1.6),[4] the relationship between the average tax rate, equilibrium output, and budget revenues shown in Figure 1.1 can be considered true only when government purchases and net taxes do not depend on each other. Naturally, in such conditions, when the average tax rate rises and is fixed, there is an outflow of some funds from economic circulation, which, all else being equal, has a negative effect on the amount of aggregate demand and causes a contraction of equilibrium output, as is shown in Figure 1.1.

[4] The assumption, all else being equal, is used to clearly establish the direction of the average tax rate's influence on aggregate demand. Meanwhile, there is extensive literature studying the effect of the tax burden and the average tax rate on the level of business activity of individual economic agents and on the amount of aggregate output (supply) as a whole (for example, Ananiashvili, & Papava, 2009, 2010b; Balatsky, 2003; Bobrova, 2005; Kochetov, 2006;).

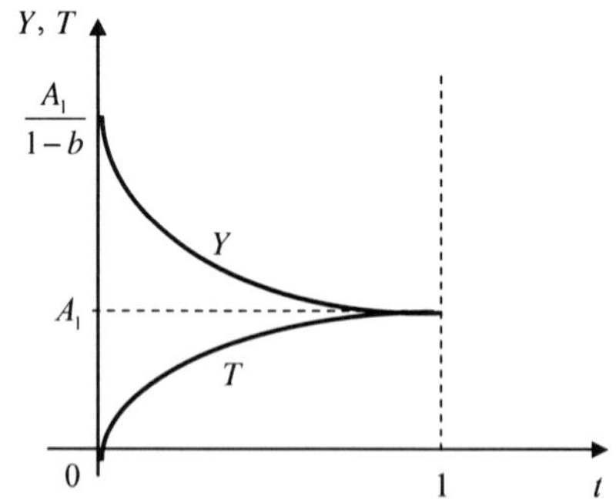

Figure 1.1. Dependence of Equilibrium Output and Budget Revenues on the Tax Rate in First Version of the Keynesian Model.

However, in reality, and are quantities that depend on each other. In practice, the value of is generally planned, for the most part, depending on what the expected net tax revenues are. Furthermore, the need for changes in the average tax rate is determined precisely by the steady growth of government purchases.[5] Hence, in the model of aggregate demand, and should be considered not as isolated from each other—as in (1.1)–(1.6)—but as related to each other.

1.2. Second Version of the Keynesian Model

We now consider the connection between government purchases (*G*) and net taxes (*T*) using an equation for the government's budget:

$$D = G + rB_{-1} - T = (G - T) + rB_{-1}, \qquad (1.10)$$

where is the amount of government debt[6] or government assets at the beginning of the period (in the case of debt, $B_{-1} > 0$; in the case of assets, $B_{-1} < 0$); is the averaged rate based on which interest payments are made at

[5] According to Wagner's law, demand for public goods rises faster than demand for private goods, which is gradually saturated. Therefore, consumers are willing to give up more and more of their income as taxes funding the production of public goods (Kolosnitsina, 2003, p. 390; Balatsky, 2012).

[6] Government debt (public debt) includes the loans taken internally in the private sector (domestic debt) and outside the country in various financial institutions and states (foreign debt).

the expense of debt or assets. Consequently, represents the amount of debt service ($rB_{-1} > 0$) or interest income ($rB_{-1} < 0$) received from payments out of assets; and is a quantity representing the budget's deficit or surplus. If in (1.10), then the budget is balanced. If $D < 0$, then the budget has a surplus. And finally, if $D > 0$, then the budget has a deficit.

In the case of a deficit budget, tax revenues are not enough to cover spending. Therefore, the government is forced to borrow an appropriate amount from the private sector, international financial organizations, other countries, or the central bank. Borrowing from the private sector is particularly common. This process is carried out directly by the state treasury, whose securities are sold to individuals, firms, commercial banks, and other financial institutions. The money obtained in this way at the expense of the state treasury is used, just the way tax revenues are, to cover government spending. Financing a deficit with credit from the private sector (*debt financing*) is the basic form of deficit financing and is widely used in most countries in the current conditions. However, there are individual exceptions, especially in developing countries, when the treasury borrows from the central bank to finance a deficit. In this case, the central bank actually purchases an appropriate part of the treasury's debt and creates "high-efficiency money" (Sachs, & Larrain, 1993,ch. 9). As we know, such financing is called *monetization of the deficit*. Without dwelling here on the positive and negative points of financing a budget deficit in these ways, we only point out that a budget cannot be constantly in deficit. There are periods when it is in surplus. In such cases, the government uses the surplus to repay or reduce the accumulated debt, or to create a reserve fund.

For simplicity, in what follows we use *D* to represent a deficit and ***B*** to represent government debt. At the same time, if necessary, we will specify the content of these quantities more precisely.

Equation (1.10) shows that the total budget deficit *D* is divided into two parts. One of them is called a *primary deficit* when it is positive, and a *positive primary balance* when it is negative (Dornbusch, & Fischer, 1990, ch. 16); and the other, rB_{-1}, is net interest payments. Representing the deficit in this form emphasizes the special significance of government debt service in budget spending. If there is debt, the interest payments necessary to service it may be so high that the budget as a whole is in deficit, even in the case of a positive primary balance.

As we see, the amount of government debt at the beginning of the period determines how much the current budget is in deficit. For its part, the budget deficit is also a basis for the origin and growth of debt. Or rather, a budget deficit in the current period fosters the growth of government debt at the beginning of the next period. In general, the following relationship is valid (for example, Blanchard, 2009, p. 579):

$$B = B_{-1} + D,$$

where B_{-1} and are the values of government debt at the beginning and end of the period, respectively.

In this relationship we take into account the value of from (1.10). Using simple operations, we get an equation that can be used to determine government debt based on the primary budget deficit as:

$$B = (G - T) + (1 + r)B_{-1}. \tag{1.11}$$

We will assume that in (1.11) is fixed and is a given quantity. This is a natural assumption, since the amount of is completely determined by decisions that the government has made in past periods. We will also assume that the value of the debt at the end of the period is exogenously planned in the government budget and, if necessary, can be changed by taking on new debt or reducing current spending. As for government purchases G, they are tied to and are determined from (1.11) as follows:

$$G = T + (B - (1 + r)B_{-1}). \tag{1.11a}$$

Consequently, we understand that the amount of government purchases is determined, on the one hand, by net tax revenues and, on the other hand, by the policy that is conducted in relation to government debt. In other words, a change in cannot be isolated—in the form in which it is traditionally considered in simple Keynesian models, including the model (1.1)–(1.6)—and it is always associated with a change in taxes or debt (or both at the same time).

We replace the condition $G = G_0$ in model (1.1)–(1.6) with (1.11a), and we call the system modified in this way *Second Version of the Keynesian Model*. The equation for calculating equilibrium output will take the following form for this model:

$$Y = \lambda_2 A_2, \tag{1.12}$$

Where

$$A_2 = a + (B - (1 + r)B_{-1}) + I_0 + NX_0, \tag{1.13}$$

$$\lambda_2 = \frac{1}{1 - b(1-t) - t}. \tag{1.14}$$

Consequently, in (1.12)–(1.14), in contrast to (1.7)–(1.9), what determines autonomous spending A_2, along with other elements, is not total government purchases G_0, but only the part of them made at the expense of government debt incurred in the current period $(B - (1 + r)B_{-1})$. According to (1.11), this quantity is determined by the primary budget deficit $(G - T)$. Moreover, in Second Version of the Keynesian Model, the autonomous spending multiplier has a completely different form. While in conditions (1.7)–(1.9) the multiplier diminishes in relation to t, the opposite situation takes place in this case, and the multiplier increases in relation to t. This circumstance leads to the following conclusions for Second Version of the Keynesian Model.

1. All else being equal, the creation or growth of government debt (creation or growth of a primary budget deficit $(G - T)$) has a positive effect on equilibrium output, while reduction of government debt or growth of government assets (creation or growth of a primary budget surplus $(T - G)$) has a negative effect. It is obvious that this situation is completely consistent with traditional Keynesian theory.
2. All else being equal, equilibrium output is an increasing function of the average tax rate t: $dY / dt > 0$. For given positive autonomous spending:

   $$Y_{min} = A_2 / (1 - b), \text{ when } t = 0; \; Y_{max} = \infty, \text{ when } t = 1.$$

   This result, which is not the customary one for Keynesian theory, is interesting from the point of view that, according to Second Version of the Keynesian Model, in conditions of insufficient autonomous spending, one of the most important ways of increasing aggregate demand and boosting economic activity is to increase the average tax rate.

3. All else being equal, net budget revenues are an increasing function of t, and for given $A_2 > 0$:

$$T_{min} = 0, \text{ when } t = 0; \; T_{max} = \infty, \text{ when } t = 1.$$

Figure 1.2 shows curves representing the dependence of and on the average tax rate in conditions of the model (1.12)–(1.14). Comparison of Figures 1.1 and 1.2 clearly indicates the difference between the results that follow from First and Second Versions of the Keynesian Model.

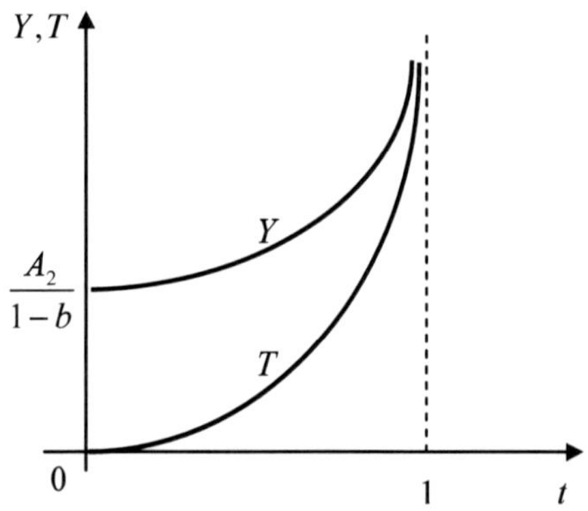

Figure 1.2. Dependence of Equilibrium Output and Budget Revenues on the Tax Rate in Second Version of the Keynesian Model.

We dwell further on an interesting result that follows from the relationship (1.12)–(1.14). In characterizing the effectiveness of fiscal policy tools, researchers often turn to the theorem of the well-known economist Trygve Haavelmo (Herr, & Kazandziska, 2011, p. 95; Matthiessen, 1966). Based on a simple Keynesian model in which taxes are determined independently of Y, the theorem asserts that the balanced budget multiplier is equal to one. In other words, according to this theorem, if the government increases its purchases and taxes by the same amount $\Delta G = \Delta T$, then output will rise by the same amount, that is, the equality will be fulfilled. It can be shown that this theorem is also valid in Second Version of the Keynesian Model.[7]

In fact, suppose that the condition takes place at the initial point of equilibrium, or, $(G-T)=0$, which is the same thing. Then we can write:

$$G=T=tY,$$

where Y, according to conditions (1.12)–(1.14), is determined by the following equation:

$$Y=\frac{A_2}{1-b(1-t)-t}=\frac{A_2}{(1-b)(1-t)}.$$

Suppose that the government has decided to increase its purchases by increasing taxes. In the context of this model, doing so entails an increase in the average tax rate by some amount Δt $(\Delta t>0,\ 0<t+\Delta t<1)$. It is easy to see that such a change in will cause a change in equilibrium output, and we get:

$$Y+\Delta Y=\frac{A_2}{(1-b)(1-t-\Delta t)},$$

where is the increase in equilibrium output. The latter can be expressed as follows:

$$\Delta Y=\frac{A_2}{(1-b)(1-t-\Delta t)}-\frac{A_2}{(1-b)(1-t)}=$$

$$=\frac{A_2\Delta t}{(1-b)(1-t)(1-t-\Delta t)}=\frac{\Delta tY}{(1-t-\Delta t)}. \quad (1.15)$$

Since $Y>0$ and $\Delta t>0$, from the derived expression it follows that the increase in output is positive.

---

[7] It is not possible to prove the validity of this theorem based on First Version of the Keynesian model, or model (1.1)–(1.6), since government purchases and taxes are not a priori interrelated in it.

We will show that $\Delta Y = \Delta T = \Delta G$. To do this, we consider the pair of equations:

$$T = tY,$$

$$T + \Delta T = (t + \Delta t)(Y + \Delta Y).$$

Subtracting the first equation from the second, we get:

$$\Delta T = t\ \Delta Y + \Delta t Y + \Delta t\ \Delta Y.$$

According to (1.15), on the right side of this expression is determined as $\Delta t Y = (1 - t - \Delta t)\Delta Y$. Taking this into account, we get $\Delta T = \Delta Y$. For its part, from (1.11a) it follows that $\Delta T = \Delta G$. Consequently, according to Second Version of the Keynesian Model, all else being equal, a tax increase fosters growth of output, but the overall effect obtained in this way is used only to provide for government purchases (the amount of household consumption remains unchanged, in spite of the growth of output; and investments and net exports are also unchanged, since, according to the assumption, these characteristics are given exogenously in the model and they are fixed). This result, together with equality (1.15), makes it possible to determine in advance how much the average tax rate should be raised in order to obtain the desired increase in government purchases without unbalancing the budget (or exceeding the planned deficit). In particular, since, all else being equal, with a tax increase, the equality will take place, from (1.15) it follows that the appropriate value of the tax increase for a given will be:

$$\Delta t = \frac{(1-t)\Delta G}{Y + \Delta G}. \tag{1.16}$$

This equation shows that the value of needed to obtain a unit increase of is variable and depends on the existing level of the average tax rate and the existing output Y. All else being equal, the higher the average tax rate or the existing output is, the less Δt can be to obtain a unit increase of G.

To clarify why equilibrium output is increasing in relation to the tax rate in Second Version of the Keynesian Model, we will first explain the principle of operation of the multiplier λ_2. We will use the standard method and consider a situation in which the amount of autonomous spending increases by one unit. This change will cause a multistage process in each stage of which the equilibrium output and the income corresponding to it will grow by a certain amount. In keeping with these stages, we will designate the value of the corresponding increases $\Delta Y^{(1)}, \Delta Y^{(2)}, \Delta Y^{(3)}$, and so on.

It is clear that for the first stage $\Delta Y^{(1)} = 1$. From this unit increase of income, will remain in the private sector, and the other part (t) will go to the government's budget in the form of taxes. In the second stage, households use the part $b(1-t)$ of their disposable income $(1-t)$ for consumption, which leads to growth of equilibrium output by the same amount. In parallel, the revenue that the budget receives goes out into the market for goods and services and increases the equilibrium output by the amount t. So in the second stage the total increase in equilibrium output will be $\Delta Y^{(2)} = b(1-t)+t$. It should be noted that, as follows from what was said above, expresses spending by households and the government to purchase products and services from a unit of income additionally created in the economy. Therefore, represents the joint marginal propensity of households and the government to purchase products and services.

Considering this circumstance, it is easy to see that for the third stage:

$$\Delta Y^{(3)} = [b(1-t)+t]\Delta Y^{(2)} = [b(1-t)+t]^2.$$

The increments of equilibrium output corresponding to subsequent stages are obtained analogously. Therefore, we will finally write:

$$\Delta Y = \Delta Y^{(1)} + \Delta Y^{(2)} + \Delta Y^{(3)} + \cdots =$$
$$= 1 + [b(1-t)+t] + [b(1-t)+t]^2 + \cdots.$$

In a normal situation, and $0 < t < 1$. On the strength of this,

$$0 < [b(1-t)+t] = [b+(1-b)t] < [b+(1-b)] = 1.$$

Consequently, the derived series is an infinitely decreasing geometric progression, and the following equality is valid:

$$\Delta Y = [1 - b(1-t) - t]^{-1} = \lambda_2 .$$

As we see, the main role in the multiplier process of creating equilibrium output is played by the joint marginal propensity of households and the government to purchase goods and services $[b(1-t)+t]$. This parameter is the weighted value of two types of marginal propensity. One of them—b—is the marginal propensity of households to consume, and the other is the marginal propensity of the government to purchase products and services. In the model under consideration, the latter is equal to one, since, according to (1.11a), each additional unit of net tax revenue is fully spent on government purchases. The two values of marginal propensity (b and 1) are weighted according to and t. Since the marginal propensity for government purchases of products and services is greater than b $(0 < b < 1)$, the greater the value of t , the higher the joint marginal propensity will be. And this means that, in the case of a high average tax rate, a large part of the income goes into the market in the form of spending and, all else being equal, the level of equilibrium output is also high.

From what has been said, it follows that when the marginal propensity of households to consume is low in a country, and government purchases are planned in accordance with (1.11a), then to stimulate aggregate demand and increase equilibrium output, it is advisable to raise the average tax rate. At the same time, it should be taken into account that implementing this measure will not affect the total amount of household consumption and will only increase the part of output that will go to providing for government purchases.

1.3. Third Version of the Keynesian Model

We consider one more version of the Keynesian model, which differs from Second Version given above in how it describes the correlation between G and T. In particular, suppose that only a certain part of the net taxes going to the budget is used for purchases, and the rest is used to service government debt and create a reserve fund. In addition, we will assume that part of the government purchases is determined exogenously and does not depend on taxes. In such conditions, the correlation between and can be expressed by the following linear function:

$$G = gT + \widetilde{G}_0, \qquad (1.17)$$

where $\widetilde{G}_0$ is the autonomous value of government purchases the amount of which does not depend on taxes and is determined exogenously. In conditions of insufficient tax revenues, this part of purchases can be made through borrowing; and is the marginal propensity for government purchases. This parameter should be seen as exogenously regulated. Based on the situation existing in the economy, the government can increase or decrease the value of g, but in any case the marginal propensity to purchase must satisfy the condition $0 \le g \le 1$, which is a fairly natural requirement.

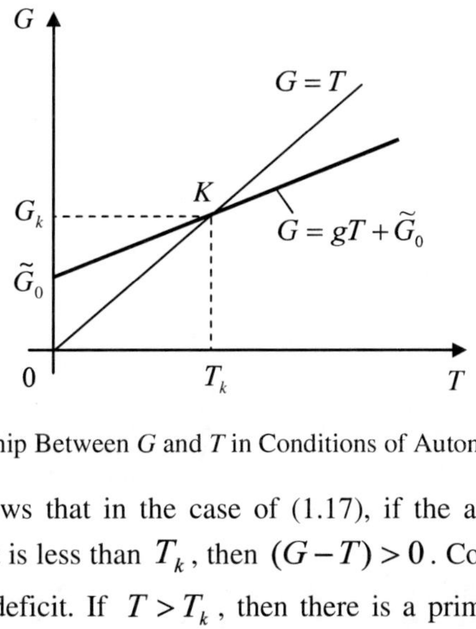

Figure 1.3. Relationship Between *G* and *T* in Conditions of Autonomous Purchases.

Figure 1.3 shows that in the case of (1.17), if the amount of net taxes going to the budget is less than T_k, then $(G-T) > 0$. Consequently, there is a primary budget deficit. If $T > T_k$, then there is a primary budget surplus (positive primary balance). And finally, a balanced primary budget is reached at the point K, at which time $G_k = T_k = \widetilde{G}_0/(1-g)$.

In model (1.1)–(1.6), we replace the condition $G = G_0$ with (1.17) and call the system thus obtained *Third Version of the Keynesian Model.* It is easy to establish that, according to this version, equilibrium output is determined by the following equation:

$$Y = \lambda_3 A_3, \qquad (1.18)$$

where:

$$A_3 = a + I_0 + \widetilde{G}_0 + NX_0, \tag{1.19}$$

$$\lambda_3 = \frac{1}{1-b(1-t)-gt} = \frac{1}{(1-b)-t(g-b)} . \tag{1.20}$$

As we see, in this model it is not the total amount of government purchases that participates in the creation of autonomous spending A_3, along with the elements a, I_0, and NX_0, as is traditional in the Keynesian model of aggregate demand, but a part of this amount $\widetilde{G}_0$: autonomous government purchases, that is, purchases whose amount does not depend on net taxes going to the budget. Consequently, the autonomous spending multiplier is also different. The latter is determined by the joint marginal propensity of households and government to purchase products and services $[b(1-t)+gt]$, which is the weighted average of and g. Comparing (1.9), (1.14), and (1.20), we notice that the multipliers and are particular cases of λ_3. Specifically, is derived from in the case when g—the marginal propensity for government purchases—is equal to zero;[8] and if in (1.20), then turns into λ_2.

Previously, when considering First and Second Versions of the Keynesian Model, it was shown that changes in the average tax rate affect equilibrium output differently in the cases when and $g=1$. Generalization of this fact gives us (1.18)–(1.20), from which it follows that in the Keynesian model the role of the average tax rate is determined by the relationship between the marginal propensity to consume b and the marginal propensity for government purchases g. When $b>g$, a rise in the average tax rate lowers the joint

[8] Zero marginal propensity to purchase does not mean that no purchases are made. The point is that the concept of marginal propensity to purchase is understood as spending on the acquisition of goods and services that the government takes upon itself from an additional unit of net taxes. Since the government can make purchases through borrowing or from nontax revenues, with a zero value of g it is entirely possible that G is positive. In model (1.1)–(1.6), as well as in the simple modification of it that is widely used in macroeconomic textbooks to illustrate the results of fiscal policy, it is actually implicitly understood that government purchases are made precisely through borrowing or from nontax revenues.

propensity of households and the government to purchase products and services $[b(1-t)+gt]$. Therefore, all else being equal, an increase in causes a reduction in equilibrium output. And in the opposite case (i.e., when $b < g$), an increase in the average tax rate causes growth of the joint marginal propensity of households and the government to purchase products and services, which, all else being equal, is a condition that fosters the growth of aggregate demand and, consequently, equilibrium output. And finally, when $b = g$, then both the joint marginal propensity of households and the government to purchase products and services and aggregate demand are indifferent to t. Figure 1.4 shows curves corresponding to equilibrium output and net budget revenues determined in relation to for Third Version of the Keynesian Model, with different possible combinations of the values of b and g. From the analysis done using the versions of the Keynesian model examined above, we can draw the following conclusion. The effect of an increase (or decrease) in the average tax rate and taxes as a whole on aggregate demand is not unequivocally negative (or positive), as it is customarily presented in canonical form in contemporary macroeconomic textbooks (for example, Blanchard, 2009, ch. 6; Dornbusch, & Fischer, 1990, ch. 3; Mankiw, 1992, ch. 9; Sachs, & Larrain, 1993, ch. 12). Depending on what the values of the marginal propensity to consume and the marginal propensity to purchase are, in the general case a tax increase can cause either a reduction or growth of aggregate demand. At the same time, since is a parameter that the government can easily regulate, by selecting its appropriate value the government can purposefully use a tax increase to conduct a stimulating or inhibiting economic policy. Suppose that the government has decided, all else being equal, to increase the tax rate by an amount Δt. We will consider how the equilibrium output Y, net tax revenues T, government purchases G, and household consumption will change in the conditions of Third Version of the Keynesian Model. As we did before, we designate the expected changes as ΔY, ΔT, and ΔC. It is easy to see that the change in equilibrium output is calculated in the following form:

$$\Delta Y = \frac{A_3}{(1-b)-(t+\Delta t)(g-b)} - \frac{A_3}{(1-b)-t(g-b)} =$$

$$= \frac{A_3 \Delta t\,(g-b)}{[(1-b)-t(g-b)][(1-b)-(t+\Delta t)(g-b)]}.$$

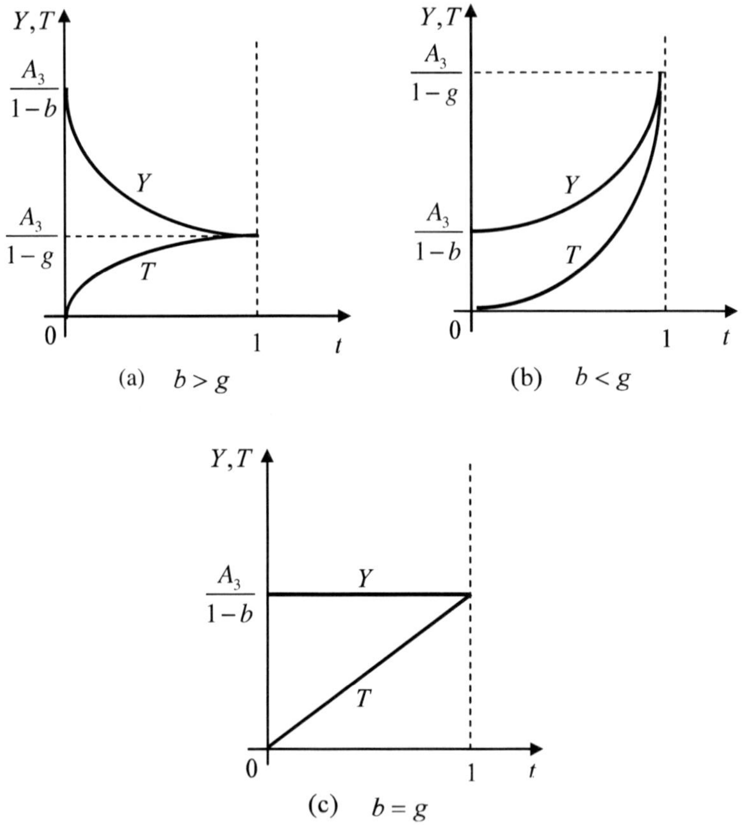

Figure 1.4. Dependence of Equilibrium Output and Budget Revenues on the Tax Rate in Third Version of the Keynesian Model.

Considering the values of from system (1.18)–(1.20), this equation can finally be written as:

$$\Delta Y = \frac{\Delta t\ (g-b)Y}{[(1-b)-(t+\Delta t)(g-b)]}\ . \tag{1.21}$$

To determine ΔT, we transform (1.21) as follows:

$$\Delta t(g-b)Y = (1-b)\Delta Y - t\Delta Y(g-b) - \Delta t\Delta Y(g-b)\,.$$

As a result of regrouping and combining similar terms, we get:

$$(\Delta tY + t\ \Delta Y + \Delta t\ \Delta Y)(g - b) = (1 - b)\Delta Y .$$

Since in the case of $g \neq b$, $\Delta T = \Delta tY + t\Delta Y + \Delta t\Delta Y$, while in the case of $g = b$, $\Delta T = \Delta tY$, the increase from net taxes has to be calculated according to the equation:

$$\Delta T = \begin{cases} (1-b)\Delta Y/(g-b), & \text{when} \quad g \neq b; \\ \Delta tY, & \text{when} \quad g = b. \end{cases} \qquad (1.22)$$

According to (1.17), $\Delta G = g\Delta T$. Consequently, the amount of increase in government purchases corresponds to the equation:

$$\Delta G = \begin{cases} g(1-b)\Delta Y/(g-b), & \text{when} \quad g \neq b; \\ g\Delta tY, & \text{when} \quad g = b. \end{cases} \qquad (1.23)$$

As for the increase in household consumption, based on function (1.2), it is calculated as follows:

$$\Delta C = b(\Delta Y - \Delta T) = \begin{cases} b(g-1)\Delta Y/(g-b), & \text{when} \quad g \neq b; \\ -b\Delta tY, & \text{when} \quad g = b. \end{cases} \qquad (1.24)$$

We will analyse equations (1.21)–(1.24) and the conclusions stemming from them. First, we call attention to (1.21). It is easy to verify that in a normal situation the value of the denominator on the right side of this expression satisfies the condition $0 < [(1-b) - (t + \Delta t)(g - b)]$. Therefore, when increases (i.e., when $\Delta t > 0$, the sign of depends on the relationship of and b:

$$\Delta Y \begin{cases} > 0, & \text{when} \quad g > b; \\ < 0, & \text{when} \quad g < b; \\ = 0, & \text{when} \quad g = b. \end{cases} \qquad (1.25)$$

Consequently, only in certain cases does an increase in cause growth of equilibrium output.[9] But then, from (1.22)–(1.24) it follows that the signs of ΔT, ΔG, and do not depend on the relationship of the parameters and b. In general, disregarding some insignificant exceptions, with an increase in net taxes and government purchases grow, and the amount of consumption decreases. More specifically, equations (1.22)–(1.24) indicate the following interesting circumstances.

First of all, if $g \neq 0$, then an increase in simultaneously causes an increase in net taxes as well as government purchases G, while if $g = 0$, then only net taxes will go up:

$$\begin{cases} \Delta T > 0, \Delta G > 0, & \text{when} \quad 0 < g \leq 1; \\ \Delta T > 0, \Delta G = 0, & \text{when} \quad g = 0. \end{cases} \tag{1.26}$$

Second, all else being equal, an increase in does not change the amount of the budget deficit (or surplus) in only one case: when the marginal propensity to purchase $g = 1$. In this case, $\Delta T = \Delta G$. With any other value of the marginal propensity to purchase, net taxes will rise more than government purchases if there is an increase in t, and this will create an opportunity to reduce the deficit (if there is one) or to create and increase a surplus:

$$\begin{cases} \Delta T = \Delta G, & \text{when} \quad g = 1; \\ \Delta T > \Delta G, & \text{when} \quad 0 \leq g < 1. \end{cases} \tag{1.27}$$

Third, it is easy to see that, all else being equal, in all cases of a change in t, the following equality is fulfilled:

$$\Delta G + \Delta C = \Delta Y, \tag{1.28}$$

in which and have different signs. In particular, when increases, then, regardless of whether is positive or negative, and $\Delta C \leq 0$. When the marginal propensity to purchase $g = 1$, the amount of consumption does not change

[9] We pointed out this circumstance previously, and therefore we do not dwell on it here. We only note that in the majority of cases g is greater than b and therefore an increase in t is one of the conditions fostering growth of equilibrium output.

$(\Delta C = 0)$, and the entire growth of output goes to government purchases $(\Delta G = \Delta Y > 0)$. When $g = 0$, the situation is directly opposite. In this case, $\Delta G = 0$, and a tax increase reduces consumption and output by the same amount $(\Delta C = \Delta Y < 0)$. From equations (1.28) and (1.25), it follows that, in the general case, with an increase in t, and are in the following relationship to each other:

$$\begin{cases} \Delta G > -\Delta C, & \text{when} \quad b < g \le 1; \\ \Delta G = -\Delta C, & \text{when} \quad g = b; \\ \Delta G < -\Delta C, & \text{when} \quad 0 \le g < b. \end{cases}$$

Consequently, when $g > b$, with an increase in t, purchases will grow more than consumption is reduced. This circumstance determines the grow of aggregate spending, as a result of which output also grows. And on the other hand, when $g < b$, consumption decreases more than purchases grow. In turn, this causes a decrease in aggregate spending and output.

Chapter 2

The Laffer Curve and its Modifications

One of the most disputable problems of the modern economic theory is that of the tax burden's impact on economic activity of people, as well as national budgetary revenues (Laffer, Moore, & Tanous, 2008).

More than four decades have elapsed since the time when an American economist, Arthur Laffer proposed a curve (later named after him) which described dependence of the national budget tax revenues on an average tax rate and according to which initially, with an increase in the average tax rate, tax revenues grow too (Laffer, & Moore, 2010, pp. 291-307); however, having reached a certain point (called a Laffer Point) at which the tax revenues reach their maximum value, they start falling. Such dependence, also known as a Laffer Effect, in some works is referred to as Laffer's Law (Guesnerie, 1998).

The Laffer Curve is the most evident illustration of the key postulations of the supply-side economics (Canto, Joiness, & Laffer, 1983). Obviously, the idea on which the Laffer Curve was based, as well as simplicity of presentation, influenced Ronald Reagan (who is said to have experienced the effects of the Laffer Curve in real life (for example, Mankiw, 2004 p. 170), a candidate for presidency at the time, so much that it became a basis of the economic policy (later called Reaganomics) which the US administration pursued after his winning the presidential election (Document, 2009; Laffer, Hass, & Pryor IV, 2009, pp. 47-77). Irrespective of skeptical attitudes of many prominent economists of the time towards the Laffer Curve itself, as well as the US position on it, clear simplicity of the graphically illustrated dependence of tax revenues on the average tax rate was gradually gaining in popularity. Later the theory of supply-side economics not only did become a subject of research on the part of the International Monetary Fund (IMF) experts (Gandhi, Ebrill, Mackenzie, & others, 1987), but one time it was recognized as a part of the IMF programs (for example, Moustapha, 1992).

Presently, almost all modern economics textbooks are evidently critical of the Laffer Curve, as well as the effects of Reaganomics (for example, Dornbusch, & Fischer, 1990, ch. 16, 18; Mankiw, 2004, ch. 8; McConnell, & Brue, 2008, ch. 15; Samuelson, & Nordhaus, 1995, ch. 17, 31). Despite this, there is a number of works aimed at studying theoretical foundations (for example, Bukach, 2011; Merkulova, 2007; Papava, 2002b, 2008; Puljic, 2006), and mathematical (for example, Guesnerie, 1998) and empirical (for example, Slemrod, 1996) implications of the Laffer Curve.

2.1. On the Foundations of the Laffer Curve

According to Evgeny Balatsky, the works devoted to the research of the Laffer Curve can be divided into two major groups and, accordingly, be classified as theoretical and practical research groups (Balatsky, 2000a, p. 33). The first group consists of works aimed at modeling fiscal and production processes and providing theoretical reasoning for parabolic curve and availability of the Laffer Points (for example, Arkin, Slastnikov, & Shevtsova, 1999; Kapitonenko, 1994; Movshovich, & Sokolovski, 1994; Sokolovskii, 1989); the other group comprises reflections on the location of the Laffer Points in different national contexts (for example, Balatsky, 1997b, 1997c, 1999, 2000a; Gusakov, & Zhak, 1995; Vishnevskii', & Lipnitskii', 2000).

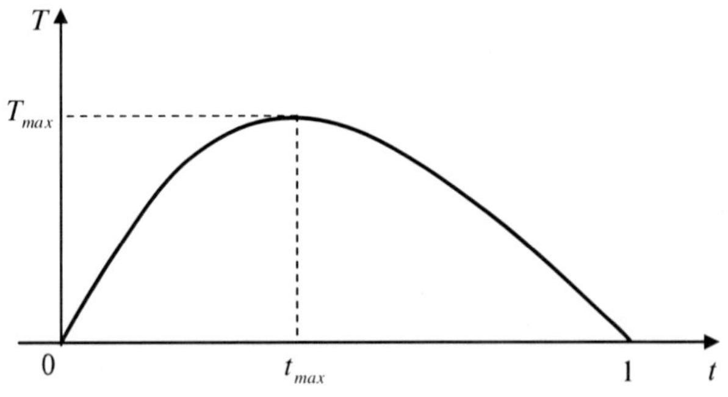

Figure 2.1. Laffer Curve.

The idea underlying the Laffer Curve is very simple: it is assumed that where the average tax rate amounts either to 0% $(t = 0)$, or to 100% $(t = 1)$, tax revenues of national budget amount to zero; however, at a certain point between 0% and 100%, where the average tax rate, or is located, the revenues reach their maximum value T_{max}. A graphical illustration of the Laffer Curve is shown on Figure 2.1.

According to Balatsky, both the idea and the graphical presentation of the Laffer Curve are based on the following purely artificial postulations:

1. A dogmatic assertion (which, in fact, is just a logical supposition) that at a certain point between 0% and 100% the average tax rate ensures a maximum amount of tax revenues (Balatsky, 1997a, p. 39); however, as is shown below, further research may shed more light on the rightness of this assertion;
2. A hypothetical reflection on certain marginal situations, as the immediate implication of zero-rate taxes is that there is no government at all (because there would be no funds to maintain the government); furthermore, a supposition that as soon as the government succeeds in collecting all revenues in their entirety, production output will start falling and the government will no longer get anything may be disproved by a long experience of command economy; from this point one can come to a conclusion that the Laffer Curve does not "cover" the whole interval [0,1], but rather a shorter section of it $(0,t_0)$, where (Balatsky, 1997b, p. 93); with this correction the Laffer Curve will look like it is presented in Figure 2.2;
3. A mechanical implication, stemming from an original macroeconomic statement of problem, that all taxes are proportional, as a result of which more sophisticated fiscal systems (of both progressive and regressive taxation), which can be encountered quite often in practice, "can not fit" an aggregated framework of the Laffer Curve (Balatsky, 1997a, pp. 39-40);
4. A supposition that there is an economy without inflation, as the Laffer Curve describes tax revenues in their nominal value; as a result, under the conditions of the Oliver-Tanzi effect which causes the growth of tax revenues, as well as the shrinking of tax base because of a relatively high inflation rate (i.e. in the environment of inflation), it becomes necessary to recalculate tax revenues in real terms; however,

this may question the very existence of the Laffer Curve, as such (Balatsky, 1997a, pp. 40-42).

It is no surprise that in view of the above-stated, as well as the results got by other researchers, Balatsky comes to a conclusion that the Laffer Curve is nothing but a beautiful hypothesis which, on the whole, has not been proved by anything (Balatsky, 2000c, p. 9). Despite this, many researchers presume existence of the Laffer Curve as something given *a priori* (for example, Aleksashenko, Kiselev, Teplukhin, & Yasin, 1989; Dagaev, 2001; Papava, 1996, 1999; Sokolovskii, 1992).

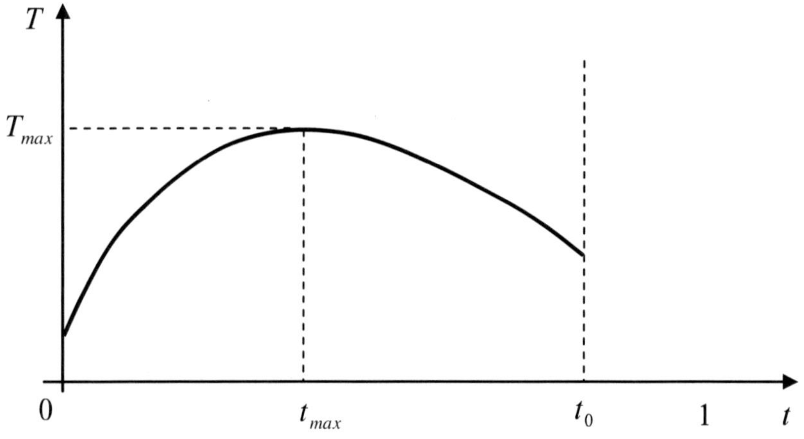

Figure 2.2. Laffer Curve under Undetermined Marginal Conditions.

A number of works are designed to determine a level of “dependence” of specific taxes on the Laffer Curve. Specifically, it is demonstrated that what this curve describes best is dependence of tax revenues on the value-added tax (VAT) rate (Gusakov, & Zhak, 1995; Movshovich, & Sokolovski, 1994); however, one has to note that applicability of the Laffer Curve to some categories of taxes is quite questionable (Balatsky, 1997a, 1997b).

In fact, since the very invention of the Laffer Curve the question of using it with the purpose of setting an optimal profit tax rate; however, as a result of the most recent theoretical studies, it was established that this curve was not usable for describing changes in the profit tax rate and that any rise in this rate would be followed with the rise in budgetary revenues as well (Movshovich, & Sokolovski, 1994, pp. 139-140).

It must be underlined that originally the Laffer Curve was formulated in a macroeconomic context, for which reason it is not applicable to individual taxes, but rather to a certain average tax rate (Balatsky, 1997a, p. 39). Quite often, instead of the average tax rate, they use the concept of "tax burden" which is described as a ratio of actual tax revenues of the national budget to a country's GDP (Balatsky, 2000a, pp. 33-34).

We believe that this method of estimation of tax burden is quite disputable, as it does not cover, on the one hand, all those potential tax revenues which, for a number of reasons, never go to the national budget, including the heavy weight of tax burden, and, on the other hand, that part of GDP which for the same reasons is produced by "shadow economy"; in other words, this index, which is designed to measure tax burden, does not cover the losses of both the national budget and the GDP and the reason for that is its heavy weight.

As was noted above, graphically the Laffer Curve is described as a "ratio of tax rate – to tax revenues". As to the idea on which the curve is based, it covers not only fiscal, but also production-related aspects of changes in the average tax rate. In particular, according to the proponents of the supply-side economics, a decrease in the average tax rate down from a relatively high point facilitates the growth in both the labor supply and investments, which in turn, brings about the growth of GDP and, in the long run, the expansion of the tax base. As Balatsky points it out, the concept of Laffer Curve rests on a belief that there is a certain dependence of tax base (in other words, of the GDP) on the average tax rate, analogous with the dependence of tax revenues on the same average tax rate; in other words, by the Laffer Curve one may describe simultaneously fiscal and production-related aspects (effects) of any changes in the average tax rate (Balatsky, 1997a, p. 39).

On the basis of this assumption, Balatsky offers to split the entire concept of the Laffer Point into *two types*: the first type encompasses the cases where the GDP accomplishes its maximum value; and the second type where the climax is reached by the national budget's tax revenues (Balatsky, 1997b, 2011). In addition, if we try to draw up the Laffer Curve on the basis of the above-mentioned tax burden, we will see that the Laffer Point of the first type will be shorter than that of the second type (it will be to the left side of the abscissa axis); in other words, the maximum amount of GDP can be reached at a lower value of tax burden which can enable maximum tax revenues to the national budget. This means that during the interval between the two Laffer Points an increase in tax revenues may be effected even under the conditions of relative drop of production output (or reduction of the GDP) (Balatsky, 2000a).

This result is in perfect harmony with the works of Alexander Dagaev, who asserts that whenever the Laffer Curve is used to describe the dependence of investments on average tax rate, it is demonstrated that the value of the average tax rate at which the maximum amount of investments is reached is lower than the other one which ensures maximum amount of collected taxes (Dagaev, 1995, 2001); consequently, during the period between these two values of average tax rate, the decrease in investments will not disable increases in tax revenues.

As one can see, the Laffer Curve is related to a number of disputable questions as to conceptual and even graphical aspects. Irrespective of skeptical attitudes towards both the Laffer Curve itself and its theoretical foundations on the part of some modern prominent economists (for example, Krugman, 1994, pp. 157-158; 1998, pp. 47-51; Stiglitz, 2003, pp. 33-34, 285-286), there is a number of applied developments, primarily in respect of post-Communist economies, which witness to existence of the Laffer Effects in the real world (for example, Balatsky, 2000a; Vishnevskii', & Lipnitskii', 2000). Although this fact cannot be used as an incontrovertible evidence of the verity of the whole curve, it does confirm that under certain circumstances there is interdependence between the growth of both tax revenues of the national budget and the GDP, on the one hand, and the reduction of relatively high average tax rate, on the other hand.

2.2. Laffer Effect in Post-Communist Economies

As was noted above, the concept of the Laffer Curve "was born" and from the very beginning was "fulfilled" in the United States as a part of Reaganomics. One of its key goals was to reduce the existing national budget deficit. However, this goal was never reached; moreover, the effect was in fact just the opposite—the deficit grew (for example, Krugman, 1994, pp. 157–58; 1998, p. 48; Naumov, 1998, pp. 106–7; 1999, p. 23; Slemrod & Bakija, 1996, p. 28; Steinmo, 1993, pp. 163–64). This had a very strong impact on the formation of a skeptical attitude toward the Laffer Curve (for example, Sokolov, 2010), which, as noted above, was also reflected in modern economics textbooks.

An empirical analysis of countries that are members of the Organization for Economic Cooperation and Development (OECD) significantly calls into question the existence of the Laffer Curve, even in those countries (for example, Leibfritz, Thornton, & Bibbee, 1997, pp. 10–11). The special studies attest, however, that high marginal tax rates and their progressive nature are negatively correlated with sustainable economic growth (Padovano & Galli, 2001).

However, a logical question arises here: are the facts that the Laffer Curve was practically disproved by the U.S. economy in the 1980s (for example, Roubini, 1997) and that empirical studies have questioned its very existence in the context of the OECD countries sufficient proof to assert that the Laffer Effect does not exist at all, even in countries that have a different economic background?

It is quite possible that the answer to this question will not be affirmative. At any rate, the question remains open in the case of post-Communist economies, because, as was noted above, some studies have shown that under certain circumstances Laffer Effects do take place (Balatsky, 2000a; Vishnevskii', & Lipnitskii', 2000). Of no less importance is the fact that Prof. Gary S. Becker in relation to Georgia (Becker, 1998) and Prof. Jeffrey Sachs in relation to Ukraine (Passell, 1996) have advocated reducing the tax burden in such countries in order to encourage both economic activities and an increase in tax revenues to the national budgets. It is noteworthy that in the Georgian context, the reduction of some tax rates in 1996, accompanied by a reduction of average tax rate as well, actually resulted in the increase of national budgetary revenues: in 1997, as a result of reducing the payment rates for the Social Welfare and Medical Insurance Fund (SWMIF) from 37 percent to 27 percent, total payments made by legal entities for the benefit of the SWMIF increased to 41 percent; incomes to the Employment Fund grew by 1 percent as a result of lowering the tax rate from 3 percent to 1 percent; budgetary revenues increased by 26.4 percent and 34.6 percent, respectively, as a result of reducing the excise tax on beer from 100 percent to 15 percent and import duties on certain goods from 12 percent to 5 percent; an "anti-example" of these was the government's decision—made under the IMF's pressure—to raise, as of January 1, 2000, the cigarette excise tax rates by 60 percent for filter cigarettes and by 110.5 percent for nonfilter cigarettes; as a result, tax revenues from the cigarette business dropped by 36.9 percent (Papava, 2003, pp. 46).

An important feature typifies economies in post-Communist transformation and distinguishes them from other economies: a post-Communist economy is characterized by a free availability of idle production capacities, as a result of which real growth of production output can be attainedwithout utilizing significant investments. This creates favorable grounds for the development of Laffer Effects (Vishnevskii', & Lipnitskii', 2000, pp. 110–11). However, here we must make a very important remark: because of their inability to produce competitive goods, many enterprises in post-Communist countries, are actually "dead," which brings about what we call *Necroeconomics* (Papava, 2002a; 2005, pp. 28-38). Obviously, "dead" enterprises cannot have production capacities, as such.

During the transition from a command economy to a market economy, even if the reduced tax burden facilitates the growth of supply, to no less an extent, it will stimulate the growth of demand as well, which may be very important for post-Communist economies. Such a transition was formulated as a theoretical postulation called the Laffer-Keynesian synthesis,[1] which forms a methodological base for "tax therapy" whose goal is to stimulate the development of post-Communist economies (Papava, 1996, pp. 263–67; 1999, pp. 285–91).

The Keynesian approach rests on the assumption that a decrease in tax rates causes an increase in consumption; in a short-term perspective, an increase in consumer spending results in the growth of demand for goods and services, in other words, of production output and employment; at the same time, a decrease in savings caused by the increase in consumption results in the intensification of competition between investors, which, in the long run, brings about an increase in interest rates; this, in turn, discourages local investors and produces incentives for foreign capital (for example, Mankiw, 1992, ch. 16). It has been argued that this effect has negative implications for countries with developed economies. However, as far as post-Communist economies are concerned, the following positive results can be expected: first, the reduction of tax burden may indirectly facilitate at least the partial utilization of the abovementioned idle production capacities, and, thereby, an expansion of production; second, the replacement of necroeconomy (Papava, 2002a; 2005) with competitive businesses can only be feasible via attracting foreign investments (Papava, 1996, p. 264; 1999, p. 287).

As was noted above, in post-Communist economies, because of readily available production capacities, the likelihood that Laffer Effects will show up grows. Nevertheless, as is shown below, this does not necessarily mean that the Laffer Curve itself exists.

[1] More details about the Laffer-Keynesian synthesis are discussed in the Chapter 4.

2.3. "Tax Hysteresis" and Modifications of the Laffer Curve

The "corrections" to the Laffer Curve are based on a factor of time, in particular, of that time interval which is necessary for the Laffer Effect to be disclosed.

Most recent studies have shown that whenever the time factor is taken into account, of no less importance is the question – in which direction the Average Aggregate Tax (average tax rate) is changing: upward (Balatsky, 2000c) or downward (Vishnevskii', & Lipnitskii', 2000). Let us review each of these scenarios separately (Papava, 2002b; 2005, pp. 109-113; 2009).

Balatsky proposes a concept of "post-effect" the key implication of which is that at a certain point, a further increase in average tax rate brings about the cutting of budget's tax revenues only after a couple of years (Balatsky, 2000 c, p. 8). Dagaev, in turn, uses a concept of tax "hysteresis" (which in Greek means "deferment") (Dagaev, 2001, p. 65). To the extent that the Laffer Effect always appears a couple of years later, a more precise phrase would be *the Laffer Effect with Tax "Hysteresis,"* or *the Laffer "After-Effects,"* or *the Laffer "Post-Effects."*

Because of a need to take into account the time factor, a so-called fiscal curve, in which this effect should be reflected, should not be expressed by "tax revenues and average tax rate" coordinates, as is the case in connection with the Laffer Curve, but rather, as is proposed by Balatsky, by those of "tax revenues and time" (Balatsky, 2000c, p. 9). We believe though that the best option would be a three-dimensional fiscal curve presented by the following three coordinates: average tax rate (t), tax revenues (T), and time (Papava, 2002b; 2005, pp. 109-113; 2009).

Before we offer a graphical illustration of the said fiscal "hysteresis" on a fiscal curve, let us consider the scenario where the average tax rate is changing upward. Bearing this in mind, let us project the said three-dimensional space (see Figure 2.3).

Let us consider the time interval $[0, \tau_2]$ during which average tax rate goes up from 0 to 1. As is shown in Figure 2.3, in case of the interval $[0, \tau_1]$, an increase in average tax rate results in the growth of tax revenues, which reach their climax at the point of t_{max}; and are relevant points on the fiscal and tax curves respectively. It is during the transition from to on the fiscal curve that Laffer Effect with the tax "hysteresis" appears, provided the average tax rate is going upwards; specifically, even at a very insignificant increase in of average tax rate, the tax revenues will start falling only after years, i.e. as of the year $(\tau_1 + \theta)$. In other words, of the fiscal curve corresponds to and of the tax curve; at the same time, the latter (i.e. D) matches of the fiscal curve.

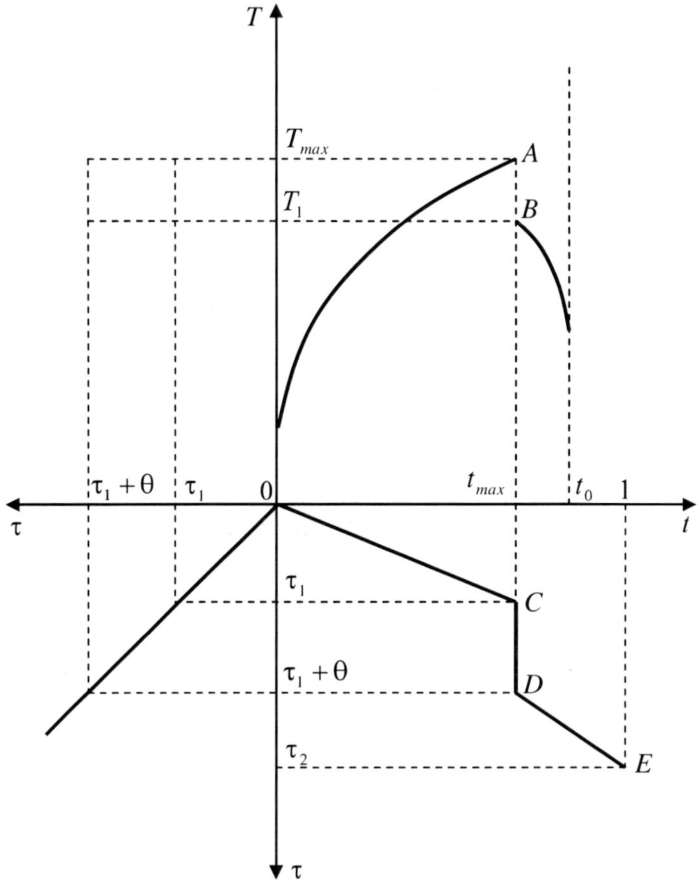

Figure 2.3. Balatsky Curve.

Consequently, if average tax rate is equal to t_{max}, in the year tax revenues will reach their maximum value T_{max}, whereas in the year they will be reduced to T_1. The split of the fiscal curve at the points and is the very reflection of the Laffer Effect with the tax "hysteresis." Please note that in case of a further increase in average tax rate, after it's "passing" the Laffer Effect with tax "hysteresis" (which on the tax curve is illustrated by a move from to E), during the interval tax revenues will be dropping.

It is noteworthy that on the fiscal curve we are considering here (Figure 2.3), the Laffer Effect looks significantly modified, which fact, as was noted above, is a result from the effect of tax "hysteresis." Furthermore, the Laffer Point is missing and the fiscal curve itself, displayed on Figure 2.3, hardly could be referred to as the Laffer Curve. To the extent that the fiscal curve on Figure 1.3 is a reflection of Balatsky's research efforts, it would be fairer to call it the *Fiscal Curve According to the Balatsky Version,* or simply the *Balatsky Curve,* and t_{max} point (for the purposes of this curve), at which the effect of tax "hysteresis" appears, the *Balatsky Point* (Papava, 2002, p. 76; 2005, pp. 110; 2009, p. 199).

The Laffer Effect with tax "hysteresis," as is shown by Vishnevskii' and Lipnitskii', reveals itself—in a somewhat modified shape though—in the case where the average tax rate is changing downwards (Vishnevskii', & Lipnitskii', 2000, pp. 113-114). Like in the case of Figure 2.3, let us draw a graphical picture of the fiscal curve, where during the time interval $[0, \tau_2]$ the average tax rate goes to 0 down from 1 (see Figure 2.4).

According to Figure 2.4, during the time interval $[0, \tau_1]$, a reduced average tax rate rate (t) causes an increase in budgetary tax revenues up to t_{max}, which revenues, having approached the level (which corresponds to on the fiscal curve), drop immediately to the level (which corresponds to on the fiscal curve) and stay there for the subsequent years (θ). Consequently, and of the fiscal curve match of the tax curve. In the year $(\tau_1 + \theta)$, however, provided the average tax rate is the same amounting to t_{max}, because of the effects of tax "hysteresis," tax revenues will "jump" to their maximum value, (which corresponds to of the fiscal curve and of the tax curve). On the fiscal curve, to the extent that the average tax rate is falling, the effect of tax "hysteresis" appears during the transition from to C, "through" B. If that process of falling goes on, after the year the tax revenues will be dropping too.

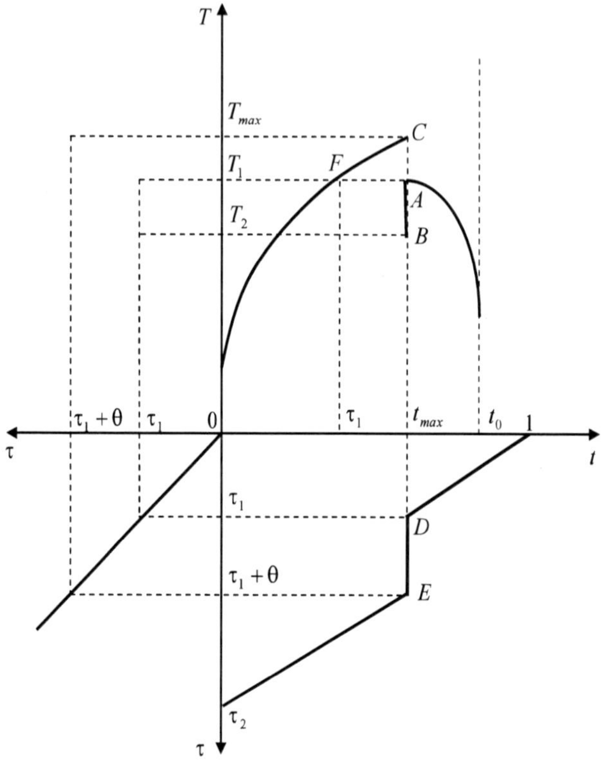

Figure 2.4.Vishnevskii'-Lipnitskii' Curve.

Like in the case of the Balatsky Curve, again because of tax "hysteresis," the Laffer Effect looks modified on this fiscal curve too (see Figure 2.4). Again, the Laffer Point is missing, for which reason one cannot call this curve the Laffer's. To the extent that the fiscal curve on Figure 2.4 is a reflection of research efforts of Vishnevskii' and Lipnitskii', it would be fairer to call it the *Fiscal Curve According to the Vishnevskii'-Lipnitskii' Version,* or sipmly the *Vishnevskii'-Lipnitskii' Curve*, and t_{max} point (for the purposes of this curve), at which the effect of tax "hysteresis" appears, the *Vishnevskii'-Lipnitskii' Point* (Papava, 2002, p. 77; 2005, pp. 112; 2009, p. 199).

The fact that both the Laffer Point and the Laffer Curve are missing does not mean that in every event of a reduced average tax rate one has to expect that a tax "hysteresis" will show up; for example, if originally the average tax rate had been in the interval and later it was cut so much that all of a sudden it was found in the interval (t_1, t_{max}), the tax revenues will grow almost "immediately" as they will be no less than T_1.

The main problem related with the practical use of the Laffer Effect is that one should not make mistake while identifying the economy's location at such section of the Vishnevskii'-Lipnitskii' Curve which corresponds to the interval (t_{max}, t_0); and further, one should not make mistake while considering to what extent an average tax rate should be cut so that to avoid an exit from the interval frame, which would mean to be between and on the Vishnevskii'-Lipnitskii' Curve (see Figure 2.4)

It happens quite often that discussions about selecting proper fiscal policies for specific countries get into difficulty because it is extremely hard to identify the exact location of economy on the Balatsky and Vishnevskii'-. Lipnitskii' Curves.

Chapter 3

IMPACT OF THE TAX BURDEN ON THE ECONOMIC GROWTH

The fact that the modern state and society could not exist without taxes needs no special proof. At the same time, it is recognized that taxation has an effect on consumption and savings, investment, supply and demand, pricing, the scale of markets, and so on (for example, Atkinson, & Stiglitz, 1980; Stiglitz, 1988). In the final analysis, all of this directly or indirectly affects the amount of production and budget revenues.

The tax burden can affect the amount of output and the budget's tax revenues in two different ways (Ananiashvili, & Papava, 2012b). On the one hand, it has an impact on production technology and the efficiency of resource use, and it influences output and budget revenues in this way. On the other hand, a change in the tax burden has an impact on the amount of use of economic resources and causes growth or contraction of production and budget revenues according to the change in the involvement of resources in production.

Two such models are presented in this Chapter. In one model, the tax burden (average tax rate) is a factor determining the technology and efficiency of resource use, while in the other it is a factor determining the amount of resource use and the level of economic activity. Both of these models consider the values of total output and budget revenues as functions depending on the aggregated tax rate. As Y is the total output, and T is the budget's tax revenues, then $Y = Y(t)$ and $T = T(t)$, where t is the aggregated (average) tax rate, which satisfies the condition $0 \le t \le 1$. In this case, it is understood that the functions and are interrelated as $T(t) = tY(t)$. This relationship shows that the behavior of the budget revenues function is substantially determined by the behavior of $Y(t)$. Therefore, of these two functions, in the models to be considered below, more attention will be given to the total output function $Y(t)$.

3.1. Transformation Model

At the theoretical level, it is rather complicated to clearly substantiate how the tax burden impacts the technological relationship that objectively exists between resource expenditures and the maximum amount of output in conditions of these expenditures. At the same time, it is absolutely logical to assume that in the same (equal) technological conditions (with the same amounts of labor and capital), a different level of the tax burden will result in a different amount of GDP (Balatsky, 2003, p. 89). The point is that, in the case of taxation, activity and individual types of products for which taxes are a considerable burden are replaced by activity and products that are less problematic from the standpoint of taxes. The return on certain alternatives for resource use declines, the return on other alternatives grows in parallel, and a new structure of production and consumption is formed, which is accompanied by redistribution of initial resources between forms of activity and a change in efficiency of the production process.

In the context of production technology, to quantitatively estimate the dependence of output on the amount of the tax burden, we can use expansions of the macroeconomic production function in which the role of the average tax rate is distinguished in some form. Such an expansion is possible in two basic directions. In one direction, taxes should be seen as a component of production technology.

If we take the Cobb–Douglas production function, for example, as the basic one, then, in this case, possible versions of its expansion by means of taxes will be:

$$Y(t) = \gamma\, Dt^{\lambda} K^{\alpha} N^{\beta}\,;\; Y(t) = \gamma\, De^{\lambda t} K^{\alpha} N^{\beta}\,,$$

where is total output; is the cost of the capital used; N is the amount of labor used; t is the aggregated (average) tax rate (the ratio of the budget's total tax revenues to GDP); e is the base of the natural logarithm (Neperian number);

D is a trend operator (a function of which the argument is time); α is the capital elasticity coefficient of output; is the labor elasticity coefficient of output; and and are parameters the statistical estimation of which, together with other parameters, is done based on time series of the variables $Y(t)$, K, N, and t.

In the second way of expanding the production function, taxes are seen not as components of technology, but as factors that act on the efficiency of technology, or rather, on the efficiency of the resources used in technology: labor and capital. We will analyse one version of such an expansion below. Suggested by Evgeny Balatsky (Balatsky, 2003, p. 88), it is a production function with variable elasticity, in the following form:

$$Y(t) = \gamma\, DK^{\alpha(t)} N^{\beta(t)}, \tag{3.1}$$

where $\alpha(t)$ and are the capital and labor elasticity coefficients of output, the values of which depend on the average tax rate t.

It should be noted that function (3.1) and the budget revenues function corresponding to it

$$T(t) = tY(t) = t\gamma\, DK^{\alpha(t)} N^{\beta(t)}, \tag{3.2}$$

as well as a model (3.1)–(3.2) was developed by Balatsky for a broader purpose than that in connection with which we are talking about it in this case: for substantiating the macroeconomic concept of the Laffer Curve and estimating the effect of fiscal policy on the level of business activity in a country with reasonable reliability (Balatsky, 2003, p. 89). In spite of this, we believe that in modeling the relationship of the average tax rate and output, even with the version of the expanded production function (3.1), it is only partially possible to reflect the essence of the Laffer concept. The point is that the underlying essence of the Laffer theory—that is, its philosophy—consists in the idea that an increase or decrease in the tax burden, by creating a negative or positive system of stimuli, fosters a decline or growth in economic activity, which is primarily expressed in a change in the amount of use of resources, rather than in an increase or decrease in the efficiency of their use. Consequently, to characterize the main aspect of the Laffer theory requires a model that is based on a behavioral equation and can reflect the positive and negative stimuli created by taxes, rather than a model based on the transformation equation (3.1), which for the most part is used to characterize production technology.[1]

Although (3.1) is not a behavioral equation that can reflect the positive and negative stimuli created by taxes, model (3.1)–(3.2), on the whole, is a tool with broad theoretical possibilities. There are two reasons for this. The first involves the specific nature of the production function itself. As we know, the Cobb–Douglas production function, on which this model is based, can be used to calculate and analyse many technical and economic characteristics (for example, Kleiner, 1986). The second reason involves consideration of the institutional factor. In particular, including the tax rate in a model of the production function and adopting the hypothesis that the tax burden has an effect on production technology and the efficiency of resource use (in our view, the model is based precisely on such a hypothesis) enables us to analyse the technical and economic characteristics obtained from a typical production function from a new angle. And this angle is expressed in the fact that all of the basic parameters to be analysed, which are obtained using a total output function (3.1) and a tax revenues function (3.2) corresponding to it, are explicitly or implicitly related to the tax burden.

It is easy to see that in model (3.1)–(3.2), the impact of the tax burden on an economic system and its characteristics is realized through the capital and labor elasticity coefficients of output and $\beta(t)$, which, according to the adopted hypothesis, are functions that depend on the average tax rate t. Therefore, characterizes the percent change in output with a one percent change in the amount of capital used in conditions of taxation at the rate t. The content of is analogous, only in this case the percent change in output is considered in relation to a one percent change in the amount of labor used in conditions of the tax rate t.

The choice of a specific type of function or should be based on general theoretical considerations, the specific nature of existing statistical data, and the possibility of adequately interpreting the results of the model that is being estimated. If we use theoretical considerations and take into account that, in addition to production-technology aspects, the model should be applicable to

[1] Several types of equations are used in the practice of mathematical economic modeling, including transformation equations and behavioral equations. A transformation equation describes the correlation between some effect on an object and the result of that effect, in a particular case, the correlation between spending and results. A production function, including (3.1) is a typical example of such an equation. On the other hand, a behavioral equation characterizes the response of an agent or agents who can make a choice to stimuli or irrational factors (for example, Johansen, 1978, ch. 4; Raiatskas, & Plakunov, 1987, ch. 3).

the analysis of certain fiscal problems, then the following functions can be deemed acceptable:

$$\alpha(t) = \alpha_0 + \alpha_1 t + \alpha_2 t^2, \tag{3.3}$$

$$\beta(t) = \beta_0 + \beta_1 t + \beta_2 t^2, \tag{3.4}$$

where and β_j, are the parameters to be estimated. In this case, it is desirable that at least one of the parameters and be nonzero (in other words, it is desirable that at least one of the functions and be quadratic).[2]

The advisability of selecting quadratic functions of the elasticity coefficients and is primarily due to the fact that in the conditions of such functions there can be a maximum point for (3.1) and (3.2) in relation to t. If these points are in the range of permissible values of the tax rate—that is, in the interval $[0, 1]$—then they can be called *Balatsky's fiscal points of the first and second kind*, since Balatsky was the first to explicitly examine these two points (Balatsky, 2000a). Here it should be noted that in his articles, Balatsky called these values of the tax rate corresponding to the maximums of output and tax revenues that are derived based on model (3.1)–(3.4) Laffer points of the first and second kind. However, in our view, this name is not entirely correct, since model (3.1)–(3.4) does not completely satisfy the postulates of the Laffer theory[3] and, most important, the basic equation (3.1) in model (3.1)–(3.4) is not a behavioral equation.

We will designate the value of the tax rate corresponding to the maximum of (3.1) as t^Y, and the value of the tax rate corresponding to the maximum of (3.2) as t^T. Then to determine we should study the equation $\partial \ln Y / \partial t = 0$, and to derive t^T, the equation $\partial \ln T / \partial t = 0$. After performing appropriate transformations in these equations, we find that Balatsky's fiscal point of the

[2] In the model analysed by Balatsky, particular cases of functions (3.3) and (3.4) were considered, in which the absolute terms α_0 and β_0 are equal to zero, but both α_2 and β_2 are different from zero.

[3] It is easy to see that, in model (3.1)–(3.4), in conditions of zero taxation, (i.e., for $t = 0$), the value of output $Y$is different from zero, and budget revenues $T$are equal to zero. For the second extreme, when there is 100 percent taxation (i.e., when $t = 1$), both output and budget revenues are different from zero and coincide with each other, while according to the postulates of Laffer theory, the condition $Y(1) = T(1) = Y(0) = T(0) = 0$.

first kind t^Y —that is, the point for which output is maximum—is determined as follows:

$$t^Y = -\frac{\alpha_1 \ln K + \beta_1 \ln N}{2(\alpha_2 \ln K + \beta_2 \ln N)}. \tag{3.5}$$

Balatsky's fiscal point of the second kind t^T corresponds to the equation:

$$t^T = \frac{1}{2}\left(t^Y \pm \sqrt{(t^Y)^2 - \frac{2}{\alpha_2 \ln K + \beta_2 \ln N}}\right). \tag{3.6}$$

Equations (3.5) and (3.6) are somewhat simplified for cases when one of the functions and is linear and the other is quadratic. If we assume that $\alpha(t) = \alpha_0 + \alpha_1 t$, then (3.5) and (3.6) will take the following forms:

$$t^Y = -\frac{\alpha_1 \ln K + \beta_1 \ln N}{2\beta_2 \ln N}\ ;\ t^T = \frac{1}{2}\left(t^Y \pm \sqrt{(t^Y)^2 - \frac{2}{\beta_2 \ln N}}\right).$$

And in the case when the labor elasticity coefficient of output is linearly determined (i.e., $\beta(t) = \beta_0 + \beta_1 t$), we get

$$t^Y = -\frac{\alpha_1 \ln K + \beta_1 \ln N}{2\alpha_2 \ln K}\ ;\ t^T = \frac{1}{2}\left(t^Y \pm \sqrt{(t^Y)^2 - \frac{2}{\alpha_2 \ln K}}\right).$$

As we see, the values of points t^Y and t^T depend on the relationship of use of capital and labor. Depending on the sign and value of coefficients α_j and β_j, $j = 1,2$, in a specific situation, for a given value of capital provision, permissible t^Y and t^T (in the interval $[0, 1]$) may or may not exist. In this case, if for a given K / N (level of capital provision) there is a permissible value of Balatsky's fiscal point of the first kind, it is the only one. As for Balatsky's fiscal point of the second kind t^T, it is easy to see that its behavior depends significantly on the behavior of t^Y. At the same time, t^T is characterized by a certain specific nature due to the existence of a radicand in

(3.6). Depending on the sign and value of the expression $\alpha_2 \ln K + \beta_2 \ln N$ for given N and K, there may not be any fiscal point t^T in the interval $[0, 1]$, there may be one such point, or there may be two. From (3.6), it follows that:

(a) When $\alpha_2 \ln K + \beta_2 \ln N < 0$, then for a given ($t^Y \in [0,1]$) there can be only one $t^T \in [0,1]$. In this case, it will satisfy the condition $t^Y < t^T$, which means that the maximum production effect will be achieved in conditions of a tax rate lower than the one at which the maximum budget revenues are obtained.

(b) When $\alpha_2 \ln K + \beta_2 \ln N > 0$, then for a given ($t^Y \in [0,1]$), either there is no real t^T, or there are two values of it, which are different from each other. In the latter case, both of them are in the interval $[0, 1]$, and their values are less than the fiscal point of the first kind t^Y: $t^T < t^Y$. It is clear that, of these two values of t^T, the one that should be considered as the fiscal point of the second kind is the global maximum point—that is, the t^T that corresponds to the highest tax revenues.

One more circumstance should be pointed out. Infinite growth of K in conditions of a given N, or vice versa, infinite growth of N in conditions of a given K, causes infinite growth in the modulus of the expression $\alpha_2 \ln K + \beta_2 \ln N$. As follows from (3.6), in this case $t^T \to t^Y$. Consequently, according to model (3.1)–(3.4), if the amount of use of some production factor grows infinitely, then the difference between Balatsky's fiscal points of the first and second kind gradually disappears.

Based on model (3.1)–(3.4), along with the fiscal characteristics t^Y and t^T, significant technological characteristics are also obtained. Among them, first of all, we should note the marginal product of capital and the marginal product of labor $MPN(t)$:

$$MPK(t) = \frac{\partial Y(t)}{\partial K} = \alpha(t)\frac{Y(t)}{K}, \tag{3.7}$$

$$MPN(t) = \frac{\partial Y(t)}{\partial N} = \beta(t)\frac{Y(t)}{N}. \tag{3.8}$$

These relationships clearly show that in model (3.1)–(3.4), all else being equal, the marginal efficiency of each factor depends not only on the amount of its use (as is customary in comparatively simple production functions) but also on the existing average tax rate t. In a normal economy, in conditions of a moderate tax burden, based on their economic content the values of the marginal products of capital and labor and should be nonnegative. The point is that (3.1), as a production function, is essentially a transformation model, and in conditions of a moderate tax burden it should reflect a well-known technological pattern: if the amount of use of a resource in production increases, all else being equal, the total output, if it does not increase, at least should not decrease. On the other hand, since we are examining the tax burden as a factor affecting the efficiency of technology, it is entirely possible that with a very high average tax rate the marginal product of a factor could turn from positive to negative.

From equations (3.7) and (3.8), it follows that the condition of simultaneous nonnegativity of and for model (3.1)–(3.4) will be observed only when the values of $\alpha(t)$ and $\beta(t)$ in the range of determination of the average tax rate satisfy the following system of inequalities:

$$\alpha(t) \geq 0, \ \beta(t) \geq 0, \ 0 \leq t \leq 1. \tag{3.9}$$

However, as practice shows, in the case of quadratic functions this condition may not always be fulfilled. To illustrate this, we turn to Table 3.1, which gives results obtained by Balatsky based on econometric versions of model (3.1)–(3.4) for the economies of Russia, Sweden, Great Britain, and the United States.[4]

According to these results, for the Russian and Swedish economies, the set of solutions of the system of inequalities (3.9) is empty, if we disregard a zero tax rate.[5] This indicates that, according to model (3.1)–(3.4), for these

[4] The intervals of nonnegativity of the coefficients $\alpha(t)$ and $\beta(t)$ for Russia, Sweden, and the United States were calculated according to data given in (Balatsky, 2003). The data used for Great Britain are from (Balatsky, 2004).

[5] We believe that, when the condition of nonnegativity of *MPK* and *MPN*is violated in an identified version of a macroeconomic production function of type (3.1), we are dealing either with incorrect identification of the model or with incorrect specification, and this

countries there is no permissible nonzero value of the tax rate for which the values of the marginal products of capital and labor will be nonnegative at the same time. In the other two countries we have a comparatively better situation. For the British economy, the set of nonzero solutions of the system (3.9) is the inequality $0 \le t \le 0.35$, and for the U.S. economy it is $0.26 \le t \le 0.33$. As we see, according to model (3.1)–(3.4), in the British economy simultaneous fulfillment of the conditions and is possible in a fairly large range of values of the tax burden. It is strange, however, that in the years for which model (3.1)–(3.4) was estimated (1983–99) the tax burden that actually existed in Great Britain was outside of this range, with the exception of certain years (in particular, 1992–94) and, for the most part, provided for positive average annual values of and $MPN(t)$.[6] It is true that the model's estimated results for the U.S. economy are free of such strange results, but even here not everything is as it should be. The problem is that, according to the econometric version of model (3.1)–(3.4) estimated for the United States, the condition of nonnegativity of is (see Table 3.1). But in this interval, is increasing in relation to t,

Table 3.1. Ranges of Nonnegativity of Elasticity Coefficients $\alpha(t)$ and $\beta(t)$

	$\alpha(t) \ge 0$	$\beta(t) \ge 0$
Russia (1989-2000)	$0.7451 \le t \le 1$	$0 \le t \le 0.7425$
Sweden (1980-1994)	$0 \le t \le 0.5785$	$0.6145 \le t \le 1$
Great Britain (1983-1999)	$0 \le t \le 0.4756$	$0 \le t \le 0.3501$
United States (1986-2000)	$0 \le t \le 0.3266$	$0.26 \le t \le 1$

and so is the labor elasticity of output $\beta(t)$, the specific form of which is $\beta(t) = 127.63t^2 - 33.18t$. It is hard to explain economically why inordinate growth of the tax burden should cause growth in the marginal product of labor.

Another example of inappropriate behavior of parameters obtained from model (3.1)–(3.4) in relation to the tax burden is the scale efficiency of

means that the given mathematical construct is not applicable to modeling of the technology corresponding to the specific data at the researcher's disposal.

[6] We should point out that in (Balatsky, 2003)," for the British economy, the set of values of the average tax rate corresponding to nonnegative values of the marginal products has a completely different form: $0.57 \le t \le 0.92$. It is clear that we are dealing with a different extreme: for simultaneous fulfillment of the conditions $MPK(t) \ge 0$ and $MPN(t) \ge 0$ there has to be an unrealistically high tax burden. At the same time, the actual value of $t$in 1983–99 was much less than 0.57 (the average value of $t$in this period was 0.363).

production ($\alpha(t)+\beta(t)$). This mathematically expresses the degree of homogeneity of function (3.1) and economically shows what happens with the average cost per unit of production with an increase in the scale of production. An increase in scale implies growth in both resources (factors) included in the model by a factor of ρ ($\rho > 1$). If the tax burden in a given economic system has a significant effect on the production technology, it is not ruled out that for various values of t all three of the cases given below may occur:

(a) $\alpha(t)+\beta(t)=1$—which means that in conditions of the given tax burden the level of efficiency does not depend on the scale of production. In this case, we say that in conditions of the given t there is a constant effect in relation to scale;
(b) $\alpha(t)+\beta(t)>1$—for all values of the tax rate for which this inequality is valid, growth in the scale of production lowers the total average cost per unit of output, that is, in conditions of the given t an increasing effect of scale is at work;
(c) $\alpha(t)+\beta(t)<1$—growth in the scale of production is characterized by decreasing efficiency for all t that are solutions of the given inequality.

We turn again to the econometric versions constructed by Balatsky for model (3.1)–(3.4) (Balatsky, 2003, 2004), and determine for what values of t the economies of Russia, Sweden, Great Britain, and the United States have a constant, increasing, or decreasing effect in relation to scale. Since the parameters of these versions were obtained for a model in which $\alpha(t)=\alpha_1 t+\alpha_2 t^2$ and $\beta(t)=\beta_1 t+\beta_2 t^2$, the degree of homogeneity ($\alpha(t)+\beta(t)$) of function (1) is determined in the following form:

$$\alpha(t)+\beta(t)=(\alpha_2+\beta_2)t^2+(\alpha_1+\beta_1)t .$$

Taking into account the specific estimated values of the parameters α_j and β_j, $j=1,2$, we find that the form of the output effect (constant, increasing, or decreasing) in relation to scale is determined by the following conditions:

- for Russia (1989–2000): $-6.32\,t^2 + 4.68\,t\ (=, >, <)\ 1$;
- for Sweden (1980–94): $-1.71\,t^2 + 0.82\,t\ (=, >, <)\ 1$;
- for Great Britain (1983–99): $-105.18\,t^2 + 38.9\,t\ (=, >, <)\ 1$;
- for the United States (1986–2000): $81.76\,t^2 - 18.76\,t\ (=, >, <)\ 1$.

From these mathematical expressions, it follows that for the Russian and Swedish economies the form of the scale effect does not depend on the amount of the tax burden. The point is that however the value of t changes in the range that is permissible for it, $0 \le t \le 1$, a decreasing effect in relation to scale is maintained in both of these countries, since for any permissible value of t the inequality is fulfilled for Russia, and the inequality is fulfilled for Sweden.

We have a completely different situation for the British and U.S. economies: in these countries, the form of the effect in relation to scale depends significantly on the value of the tax rate. For example, in the British economy there is a constant effect of scale when the average tax rate is 0.0278 and 0.3421, a decreasing effect when $0 \le t < 0.0278$ and $0.3421 < t \le 1$, and, finally, an increasing effect when $0.0278 < t < 0.3421$. And in the U.S. economy we have the following pattern: is a constant effect, is a decreasing effect, and is an increasing effect.

As we see, according to the econometric models constructed by Balatsky, the British and U.S. economies differ considerably from each other in the structure of distribution of taxes determining the form of their effect in relation to scale: the switch from one form of the scale effect to another occurs in conditions of a completely different tax burden. There is nothing unexpected in this, but it is strange that in the United States an inordinate increase in the tax rate is a condition for growth of the efficiency of scale. In particular, as the results given above show, the scale effect becomes increasing only when the tax burden in the U.S. economy exceeds approximately 27 percent[7] and continues to grow to the 100 percent level that is theoretically permissible for it. It is hard to find any valid explanation of this fact. Presumably it is a manifestation of imperfection of the model's specification or identification.

In spite of individual contradictions revealed in the process of analysis of econometric versions of model (3.1)–(3.4), there is no doubt that model estimation and analysis of the tax burden's effect on existing technological

[7] In 1986–2000, the average annual aggregated tax rate in the United States varied in the range of $0.27 - 0.31$.

relationships between total production and the amount of capital and labor used in production is possible. The Cobb–Douglas function may not prove to be suitable for describing these relationships in all cases, even in the generalized form in which it is presented in model (3.1)–(3.4), and it may be necessary to use another, more complex production function.[8] But even when model (3.1)–(3.4) is satisfactory, from both the standpoint of formal statistical criteria and the standpoint of being able to interpret the results, it only partially reveals the role that taxes play in the economy. We have indicated above that the tax burden has an impact on production technology as well as on economic activity and the level of use of existing resources. We believe that this last circumstance is much more important from a macroeconomic point of view, and therefore primary attention should be given to it in modeling fiscal aspects and examining the role of taxes.

3.2. Behavioral Model

We can base the construction of this type of model on a generalized version of the concept of one of the representatives of Arthur Laffer's economic theory of supply, according to which the aggregated (average) tax rate has an impact on total output in approximately the same form as on the amount of the budget's tax revenues (Sachs, & Larrain, 1993, ch. 7). Postulates of this concept can be formulated in a formalized way as follows[9]:

1. At the extreme points and of the range of determination of the average (aggregated) tax rate, the values of total output and budget revenues are equal to zero, that is:

$$Y(0) = Y(1) = 0,\ T(0) = T(1) = 0;$$

2. There are values and of the average tax rate t such that increases in the interval and decreases in the interval $(t^*, 1]$, and increases in the interval and decreases in the interval $(t^{**}, 1]$. In this case:

[8] The Cobb–Douglas function is a good tool for theoretical analysis; however, practice shows that, even with constant elasticity coefficients, in the conditions of specific data it is often unsuitable for modeling production technology.

[9] Also see Chapter 2.

$$\max_{0 \le t \le 1} Y(t) = Y(t^*), \quad \max_{0 \le t \le 1} T(t) = T(t^{**}).$$

The average tax rate at which output is maximum is called *the Laffer Fiscal Point of The First Kind*, and that produces the maximum budget revenues is called *the Laffer Fiscal Point of the Second Kind.*[10] It is clear that of the two points the more important one for the economy is the point of the first kind t^*. Therefore, we arbitrarily call t^* *the optimal tax rate.*

The peculiarity of the function of total output with respect to the average tax rate noted here can be explained by means of the sum of positively and negatively operating effects. Positive is the effect which, in increasing of average tax rate, is contributing to economic activity and totaloutput, and in decreasing it becomes a hindering factor. Accordingly, negative are the effects which, in increasing of average tax rate, reduce economic activity and totaloutput, and in reducing of average tax rate—increases them.

The effect creating economic environment and the effect of incomes can be qualified for the **group of positive effects**. **The effect creating economic environment** purports, that the increase of the average tax rate expands financial opportunities of the government, and it carries out the economic functions assigned to it in better way. This effect is positively reflected on the aggregate supply as in the conditions of increased tax incomes, first, the aggregate supply grows actually from side of the public sector by creation of greater volume of production and services, and secondly, the government improves business-environment that is very important for contributing to the increase of aggregatesupply of a private sector.

The effect of incomes reflects direct influence of taxes on individuals' behavior. According to Atkinson and Stiglitz, **the effect of incomes** arises because collection of taxes incurs reduction of individuals incomes, they really get poor and are forced to postpone the term to retire on pension, to reduce a free time due to the increase of working hours, etc. (for example, Atkinson, & Stiglitz, 1980, ch. 2). Proceeding from such logic, the effect of incomes, in increasing of taxes, is a contributing factor to economic activity.

The replacement effect and financial effect[11] belong to **the group of negative effects or the effects of tax burden.** The Existence **of replacement effect** in relation to taxes is conditioned by the fact that not all activities are

[10] In the general case, these points are different from Balatsky's points of the first and second kinds. This will be discussed below in detail.

[11] These two effects, along with the effect of incomes, are considered as the main characteristics of taxes (Atkinson, & Stiglitz, 1980, ch. 2).

subject to taxation and what is taxed, as a rule, they are taxed at different rates. When taxes increase, under the influence of replacement effect, the economic activities pass from taxable sphere to the non-taxable sphere or from the sphere of high taxes to the sphere of low taxes. Individuals actively seek the ways, and frequently they find them that gives opportunities to evade taxes in full or in part. The ways of evading taxes leads us to the reduction of economic activity. The same result is yielded from **financial effect**. This effect arises when the same activity can be paid in different forms and, accordingly, tax rates can be different. The classical example of this financial effect is the case when, to avoid high taxes, the use of cash payments among economic subjects and passage to "shadow" economy is realized.

Proceeding from specificity of the discussed effects, it is possible to assume, that, within the frameworks of the supply-side economics, for the value of the average tax rate from 0 up to t^* the sum of the effect of economic environment and the effect of incomes (the effect positively influencing the aggregate supply) exceeds the sum of the effect of replacement and financial effect (the effect negatively influencing the aggregate supply). As a result of this the total effect of average tax rate is positive and in the given interval $dY/dt > 0$. The opposite ratio of positive and negative effects arises for the subsequent values of the average tax rate, i.e., in the $(t^*, 1]$ interval the total effect having impact on the aggregate supply, is negative: $dY/dt < 0$.

Determination of the fiscal points t^* and t^{**} can be one of the conditions fostering improvement of a country's economic policy. Two circumstances should be taken into account when constructing an appropriate model. The first one is that, in any economy, the total output depends on the amount and quality of existing economic resources (labor, capital, land, and production capabilities) and on the level of technology for using these resources. These factors determine the economy's production-technology capabilities, and if they are distributed in the best possible way and fully used we have the maximum output, which is also called *the potential output level*. The second circumstance is that no less a role in the economy is played by the institutional environment, creation of which is a function of the government. Depending on how ideal the institutional environment is, in conditions of the same production-technology capabilities, the amount of output will be different for any two economies or any two periods of time. In the case of the best, that is, ideal, institutional environment, the actual and potential outputs are equal to each other. However, as a rule, the actually existing institutional environment differs from its ideal version in most cases. Therefore, the actual level of the economy's total output is less than the potential level. Without question, an important role in creating the institutional environment is played by the tax system, along with a set of other factors. At the level of a model, we can set up a situation and assume that it is the tax system that is the main factor in creating the institutional environment that determines the behavior of economic agents. If we make such an assumption, then the total output function can be represented in the following form:

$$Y(t) = Y_{pot} f(t), \tag{3.10}$$

where is the result expressing the economy's production-technology capabilities; and is the function reflecting the institutional aspect.

From a formal point of view, represents the maximum value of any macroeconomic production function in conditions of the optimal institutional environment. More specifically, expresses the amount of potential output in conditions of the existing technology with full use of economic resources.

As for the function in (3.10), it describes the overall effect of taxes on total output. It is a behavioral function that, based on its content, should have the following properties:

1. $f(t)$ is increasing in the interval and decreasing in the interval $(t^*, 1]$. In other words, from to an increase in the tax rate fosters an improvement of the institutional environment and growth in economic activity, while from to an increase in the tax rate leads to deterioration of the institutional environment and a decline in economic activity;
2. For the optimal tax rate, $f(t^*) = 1$. This very important property indicates that the average tax rate makes it possible to create an institutional environment in which the technological aspects of production completely determine the efficiency of output. Consequently, with the optimal average tax rate, output is maximum, and (3.10) takes the form: $Y(t^*) = Y_{pot}$;
3. It is desirable for to have one more property. In particular, in the absence of taxes, that is, when $t = 0$, $f(0) = 0$, while if the profit that is made is completely confiscated in the form of taxes, that is, if $t = 1$, then $f(1) = 0$. However, it should be noted that may not satisfy the third property, fully or partially. For example, for the case $t = 0$, will be different from zero if we suppose that there are state-

owned firms and the government performs economic functions based on income received in the form of dividends from their profits.

We give an example of a total output function corresponding to (3.10), in which has the properties enumerated above. For this purpose, we use a modified version of the entropy function $(-t\ln t)$:[12]

$$f(t) = -et^{\delta}\ln t^{\delta}. \qquad (3.11)$$

Then we have:

$$Y(t) = Y_{pot}f(t) = Y_{pot}(-e\,t^{\delta}\ln t^{\delta}), \qquad (3.12)$$

where δ is a statistically estimated positive parameter; and e is a Neperian number (base of the natural logarithm).

The budget revenues function corresponding to (3.12) has the following form:

$$T(t) = tY(t) = tY_{pot}f(t) = Y_{pot}(-e\,t^{\delta+1}\ln t^{\delta}). \qquad (3.13)$$

It can be shown that, in the conditions of model (3.12)–(3.13), the values of the Laffer fiscal points of the first and second kind, t^* and t^{**}, are determined as follows:

$$t^* = \exp\left(-\tfrac{1}{\delta}\right) = e^{-1/\delta},\ t^{**} = \exp\left(-\tfrac{1}{(\delta+1)}\right) = e^{-1/(\delta+1)}. \qquad (3.14)$$

In addition, the following conditions are valid:

$$\lim_{t\to 0} f(t) = 0,,\ f(1) = 0.$$

[12] It should be noted that the entropy function was first used for illustrating the Laffer theory by V. Papava (see Papava, 1996, p. 266; 1999, p. 288). This model was later generalized by G. Loladze (Loladze, 2002).

Therefore, for the total output function (3.12) we have:

$$\lim_{t\to 0} Y(t) = 0\,,\ Y(t^*) = Y_{pot},\ Y(1) = 0\,.$$

And for the budget revenues function (3.13):

$$\lim_{t\to 0} T(t) = 0\,,\ T(t^{**}) = \frac{\delta}{1+\delta} Y_{pot},\ T(1) = 0\,.$$

As we see, in the conditions of model (3.12)–(3.13), the value of the fiscal characteristics t^* and t^{**} depend completely on parameter δ. To estimate the latter and, consequently, to identify model (3.12)–(3.13) we need observation data in relation to total output $Y(t)$, the tax rate t, and the potential output level Y_{pot}. The last of these, Y_{pot}, is not observable, that is, it is a latent quantity. Therefore, determining (estimating) its value requires developing a definite procedure, which is a separate problem.[13]

To solve the problem involving Y_{pot}, in model (3.12)–(3.14) we have to keep in mind that the potential output level Y_{pot}, in contrast to the actual level, is determined by the amount of economic resources that exist but are not used. If we take only two aggregated resources into account—labor and capital—then we can write

$$Y_{pot} = \varphi(\Phi, L)\,, \tag{3.15}$$

where Φ is the existing amount of capital; L is the existing amount of labor; and is some function that can be estimated, which can arbitrarily be called the technological function of potential output. This function cannot be estimated in isolation, by examining the expression only, since, as we pointed out above, we do not know the values of in it. At the same time, if the value of in the total output function (3.10) is replaced by the function and the expression obtained

$$Y(t) = \varphi(\Phi, L) f(t) \tag{3.16}$$

[13] In practice, several approaches are used for estimating the potential output level. For a general survey of these approaches, see (Mishkin, 2007). Some specific methods for estimating the potential output level are suggested in (Ananiashvili, 2010; Balatsky, 2000b).

is transformed into a regression equation, then, along with we can also estimate $\varphi(\Phi, L)$.

To illustrate this, we turn to statistical data that exist for the U.S. economy and consider 1970–2008 the period to be analysed.[14] To determine the specific econometric form of (3.16), we represent the potential output function (3.15) as follows:

$$Y_{pot(i)} = Ae^{\lambda i} L_i^{\mu} L_{i-1}^{\eta} Y_{i-1}^{\theta}, \tag{3.17}$$

where i is the time index; $Y_{pot(i)}$ is potential output in period i; A, λ, μ, η, and are parameters that can be statistically estimated; L_i, and are the amount of labor in periods i and $i-1$, respectively; and is actual output in period $i-1$.

Several circumstances determined the choice of such a structure for the potential output function. The first one involves overcoming the problem of autocorrelation. The lag variables (L_{i-1} and Y_{i-1}) are included in the model mostly for this purpose, although taking these variables into account expands the context of economic analysis, since it becomes possible to reflect dynamic aspects. The second circumstance involves reflection of the existing amount of capital. As we see, this factor of production, in contrast to labor, does not figure in the model in an explicit form.[15] Calculations have shown that, if the amount of capital is taken into account, some of the model's estimated parameters become statistically insignificant. Therefore, it is desirable to limit ourselves to just one basic factor: labor. What is more, even if there is no strictly econometric problem, it is justified to consider only labor as the main factor determining the potential output level. The point is that for the U.S. economy (and not only for it) labor is in shorter supply than capital. According to various calculations, for the United States the "natural" rate capacity utilization is approximately 82 percent (Corrado, & Mattey, 1997; Emery, & Chang, 1997; Garner, 1994; McElhattan, 1985),[16] while the natural rate of unemployment is less than 6 percent.

We incorporate (3.17) into (3.12), so that

---

[14] The data are taken from the official Web site of the U.S. Bureau of Economic Analysis (www.bea.gov).

[15] Although it is indirectly manifested in certain ways in the elements $A$and Y_{i-1}.

[16] See also (IMF, 2005, p. 6).

$$Y_i(t) = Y_{pot(i)} f(t_i) = Ae^{\lambda i} L_i^{\mu} L_{i-1}^{\eta} Y_{i-1}^{\theta} (-et_i^{\delta} \delta \ln t_i) \qquad (3.18)$$

and by taking the logarithm we transform this expression into a regression equation with the following form:

$$\ln\left(\frac{Y_i(t)}{-e\ln t_i}\right) = \ln(A\delta) + \lambda\, i + \mu \ln L_i + \eta \ln L_{i-1} + \theta \ln Y_{i-1} + \delta \ln t_i + \ln \varepsilon_i, \qquad (3.19)$$

where ε_i is a random term characterizing the part of the actual output's deviation from the potential level that is determined by so-called nontax circumstances. The results of estimation of this equation are given in Table 3.2. As we see, all of the model's estimated coefficients and the absolute term are statistically significant. The regular and adjusted coefficients of determination are highly significant. And there is no autocorrelation problem (it is denied by the Durbin*h*-test, at both the 5 percent and 1 percent significance levels). Consequently, the estimated model is suitable for drawing certain conclusions.

Based on the given in Table 3.2, using equations (3.14), it is easy to establish that for the period being analysed:

$$t^{*} = 0.3162,\ t^{**} = 0.5856.$$

Table 3.2. Results of Estimation of Regression Equation (3.19)

Period Analysed, 1970–2008					
Variables	**Co-efficients**	**Estimates**	**Standard Errors**	**Student's *t*-Test**	**Probability**
cons	$\ln(A\delta)$	4.1663	1.1740	3.5486	0.0012
i	λ	0.0168	0.0042	4.0091	0.0003
$\ln L_i$	μ	2.2793	0.5945	3.8342	0.0005
$\ln L_{i-1}$	η	–2.1935	0.5703	–3.8465	0.0005
$\ln Y_{i-1}$	θ	0.4334	0.1259	3.4435	0.0016
$\ln t_t$	δ	0.8685	0.0839	10.3453	0.0000
$R^2 = 0.9985$, adjusted $R^2 = 0.998$, $F(4.34) = 4{,}390$, $p < 0.0000$; $DW = 1.5770$, $h = 1.65$					

This result indicates several interesting things to us.

First, the derived value of the Laffer fiscal point of the first kind, that is, the optimal tax rate t^* is somewhat higher than the actual value of t for each year over the course of the period under consideration.[17] We can judge the results of the tax burden's deviation from the optimal rate in individual years according to the value of the function As we have indicated above, $f(t^*)=1$, and $f(t)<1$ for any $t$different fromdifferent from t^*. In the latter case, the actual output level lags behind the potential output level, and the reason for this lag may be either an excessive or insufficient tax burden. At the same time, the more the actual tax rate differs from its optimal value, the greater the difference $1-f(t)$, that is, the percent difference between the potential and actual outputs. A graphic illustration of this is given in Figure 3.1, which shows the dynamics of percent values of the lost GDP due to nonoptimality of the tax burden. Figure 3.1 shows that, according to model (3.12)–(3.13), if the Laffer theory is correct, there was a certain resource in the U.S. economy for increasing output by optimizing the tax burden. Because of the low tax burden, this resource was greater than 1 percent in some years (1971, 1975, 1983, 1984, and 2003), and less than 0.2 percent in other years. If we calculate the average value during the period, we find that in 1970–2008 the average annual lag of actual output behind the optimal level due to a nonoptimal tax burden was 0.66 percent. This is a considerable reserve, and therefore it may be said that during the period under consideration, on average, the U.S. economy functioned in conditions of a nonoptimal tax burden.

Second, the values of the Laffer fiscal points of the first and second kinds, $t^*$and t^{**}, determined according to model (3.12)–(3.13) are somewhat higher than the average values for the period of Balatsky's fiscal points of the first and second kinds, t^Y and t^T:

$$\bar{t}^Y = \frac{1}{n}\sum_{i=1}^{n} t^Y{}_i = 0.2839,\ \bar{t}^T = \frac{1}{n}\sum_{i=1}^{n} t^T{}_i = 0.2934,$$

which are determined based on model (3.1)–(3.4) (Balatsky, 2003).

[17] For reference, the actual values of t in 1970–2008 satisfied the inequality $0.2605 \le t \le 0.3028$, and the average value of $\bar{t}$ for the period was 0.2772 .

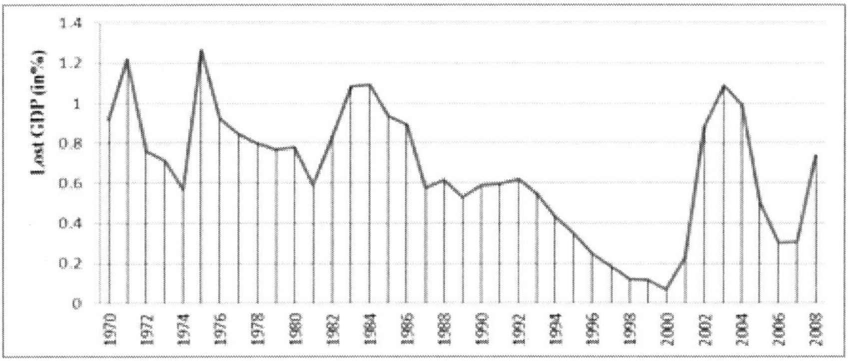

Figure 3.1. Dynamics of Deviation of Actual Output Level Behind Optimal Level Due to Nonoptimality of the Tax Burden in the United States in 1970-2008.

This is to be expected because model (3.12)–(3.13) examines the role of taxes from a broader perspective than model (3.1)–(3.4). The difference is that Balatsky's point of the first kind t^Y shows what the tax rate should be in order to get the maximum output from the economic resources included in production (those that are actually used), while the Laffer point of the first kind expresses the tax rate at which the maximum output is obtained from existing economic resources (those that can potentially be used).

Analogously, Balatsky's point of the second kind t^T is the tax rate corresponding to the maximum budget revenues in conditions of the resources that are already being used, while the Laffer point of the second kind is the same thing in conditions of the economic resources that can potentially be used. In other words, the amount of economic resources used for Balatsky's points is given, while the Laffer points should determine this amount themselves.

Third, no less attention should be given to the circumstance that the Laffer fiscal points and differ significantly from each other: according to the results obtained, t^{**} is 0.5856, almost twice as great as t^*. At the model level, we can determine what would have happened with the U.S. economy in the period under consideration if the average tax rate had been raised from the actual average value for the period to 0.5856.

According to the model, the average tax rate for period corresponds to a lag of approximately 0.7 percentage points behind the potential output. All else being equal, increasing the tax rate to 0.5856 would have increased this lag to 20 percent. This casts doubt on the advisability of an economic policy in which the government's priority is to maximize the budget's tax revenues.

We consider it necessary to make one extremely important clarification. We have in mind that the deviation of the actual output from the potential output may be caused by the effect of a nonoptimal tax burden or by other, nontax circumstances and factors.

The function reflects only the part of the deviation that is due to the tax burden. The rest of the deviation, which is due to nontax circumstances and factors, is characterized by the random term ε in equation (3.19). The effect of these circumstances and factors on the amount of output is sometimes more substantial than the effect of the tax burden, and they may work in completely opposite directions. This is confirmed by Figure 3.2, which shows the dynamics of percent values of the overall deviation of actual output from the potential output estimated according to model (3.19). As the figure shows, in individual years the deviation from the potential was three or more percentage points, while the maximum deviation because of the nonoptimal tax burden was approximately 1.2 percent.

Moreover, in individual years the effect of nontax circumstances was so strong that it exceeded the negative stimuli due to nonoptimality of the tax burden, and the actual output, instead of lagging behind, exceeded the potential output. In Figure 3.2, such cases correspond to negative values of the deviation.

Along with the curve for the dynamics of deviations of actual output from the potential output, Figure 3.2 also shows the curve for the dynamics of the actual unemployment rate. As we see, the movements of these two curves are very similar to each other, which indicates that in conditions of high unemployment the lag behind potential output was accordingly high, while in the case of especially low unemployment rate (less than 6 percent), actual output exceeded the potential.

This result should be especially emphasized, since in the proposed model neither the unemployment rate nor the amount of labor used are entered as exogenous variables. Moreover, model (3.12)–(3.13) makes it possible to endogenously estimate the value of the natural rate of unemployment (the level of unemployment existing in the conditions of potential output). To do this we must turn to a version of Okun's equation (Okun, 1962, 1970),[18] which establishes the correspondence between the unemployment rate and the amount of lost GDP:

[18] See also (Knotek, 2007; Lee, 2000; Thirlwall, 1969; Thirlwall, & Ireland, 1970).

$$\frac{Y_{pot(i)} - Y_i}{Y_{pot(i)}} = \rho(u_i - u^*), \quad (3.20)$$

where u is the existing (actual) unemployment rate; is the natural unemployment rate; and is Okun's coefficient. The latter shows the percent change in the lag of actual output behind potential output in the case of a deviation of the actual unemployment rate from its natural rate by one percentage point.[19] It is easy to see that expression (3.20) describes a static phenomenon (all of the parameters entering into it are for the same period), and therefore we can call a static Okun coefficient.

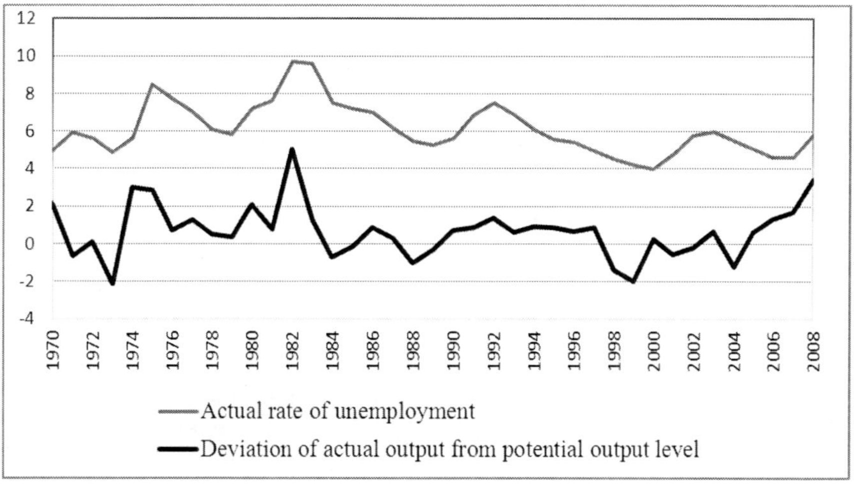

Figure 3.2. Dynamics of Deviation of Actual Output from the Potential Output Level and Unemployment in the United States in 1970-2008 (in %).

Introducing the notations $g_{pot} = (Y_{pot} - Y)/Y_{pot}$ and $\rho_0 = -\rho u^*$, we transform (3.20) into a regression model:

$$g_{pot(i)} = \rho_0 + \rho u_i + v_i, \; i = 1,2,\cdots,n, \quad (3.21)$$

[19] ρ is not the unemployment elasticity coefficient of lost GDP.

where is a random term. We estimate parameters and so that in (3.21) the values of the deviation of actual output from potential output determined by equation (3.19), are considered to be the values of the dependent variable g_{pot} . As a result of these procedures, in our case we get:

$$\begin{array}{lll} \hat{g}_{pot} = -2.4375 + 0.5049\, u \\ (s.e.) \quad (0.9499) \quad (0.152) \end{array}, \; R^2 = 0.2306;\; F(1.37) = 11.2;\; DW = 1.663,$$

where the standard errors are indicated in parentheses under the coefficients. The estimated equation is statistically significant by all criteria, and therefore, according to the data for the United States in 1970–2008, the Okun coefficient is $\rho = 0{,}5049$. Consequently, an increase (or decrease) in actual unemployment rate by one percentage point in comparison with its natural rate causes an increase (or decrease) in the amount of lost GDP by an average 0.5 percent. The value of the natural unemployment rate is 4.8274 percent and is derived from the equation $\rho_0 = -\rho\, u^*$, in which $\rho = 0.5049$, and $\rho_0 = -2.4375$.

The version of Okun's equation (3.20) differs from the one that is widely used in contemporary macroeconomics textbooks to illustrate the following version of Okun's law:

$$u_i - u_{i-1} = -\beta(g_{yi} - g^*), \tag{3.22}$$

in which represents the normal growth rate of GDP (the growth rate corresponding to a constant unemployment rate); is the actual GDP growth rate: $g_{yi} = (Y_i - Y_{i-1})/Y_i$; is Okun's parameter, which in this case expresses the effect of the amount of deviation of the actual GDP growth rate from the normal rate on the change in the unemployment rate. It is obvious that (3.22) describes a dynamic phenomenon, since the characteristics entering into it, both of the growth rate and the unemployment rate, express a change in time.

Based on this, we can call β a *dynamic Okun coefficient*. The difference in content of the static and dynamic Okun coefficients is obvious; it is also not surprising that there is a quantitative difference between them. We can easily ascertain this if, using the notations $\Delta u_i = u_i - u_{i-1}$, $\beta_0 = \beta g^*$, we transform (3.22) into the following regression model:

$$\Delta u_i = \beta_0 - \beta\, g_{yi} + \upsilon_i,\; i = 1, 2, \cdots, n,$$

where is a random term. Estimating the quantities and based on data from the same period that was used for model (3.21), we get:

$$\Delta\hat{u} = 1.2519 - 0.4024 g_y, \quad R^2 = 0.7404; \; F(1.37) = 105; \; DW = 1.788.$$
$$(s.e) \quad (0.140) \qquad (0.039)$$

It follows from this that the dynamic Okun coefficient $\beta = 0.4024$, and the normal GDP growth percent.[20]

In summary, we note that the model considered here for estimating the effect of the tax burden on the amount of resource use has worked fairly well in regard to data on the U.S. economy. The results obtained are entirely plausible in an economic sense. When different versions of the calculations were carried out, the estimated model as a whole, as well as its parameters, maintained its stability and did not lose its statistical significance in a fairly broad range of changes in the "sample size." It is interesting that, even when the quality of the model deteriorated (the parameters being estimated became statistically insignificant) as a result of excessive reduction of the sample size, the estimates of the fiscal characteristics t^* and t^{**} changed only slightly. Naturally, all of this is not sufficient grounds for drawing final conclusions about the suitability of the suggested model for conducting specific applied calculations. However, we do believe that, after some future improvements and testing of its performance with statistical data from various countries, the suggested approach may prove to be perfectly acceptable for estimating the efficiency of fiscal policy.

[20] These results are completely consistent with the data given, for example, in Olivier Blanchard's well-known macroeconomics textbook (Blanchard, 2009, pp. 184–85). Note that in some economics textbooks, including those on macroeconomics, the results obtained from the dynamic version of Okun's equation (3.22) are presented without any qualifications as the results of the static version of Okun's equation (3.20), which is incorrect, in our opinion.

Chapter 4

FOUNDATIONS OF LAFFER-KEYNESIAN SYNTHESIS

In contemporary economic theories, the role of taxes, unfortunately, is studied one-sidedly. Keynesianism mostly emphasizes the mechanisms by which taxes affect the economy through aggregate demand and almost does not take into account the mechanism of their effect on the aggregate supply side. In other words, Keynesian models consider a situation in which aggregate supply does not depend on taxes, while aggregate demand, especially the part of it that involves consumption, is a function of taxes. The problem of taxes is also seen one-sidedly by supply-side economics, in which the effect of the tax rate on aggregate supply is brought to the fore. The role of taxes can be fully explained, and the one-sided nature of these two theories can be overcome through a synthesis of supply-side economics and Keynesianism, which was first suggested by one of the present authors (Papava, 1996, pp. 263-267; 1999, pp. 285-289).

The model presented below is a further development of this idea of a Laffer-Keynesian synthesis (Ananiashvili, & Papava, 2012a). It is based on a macroeconomic equilibrium model that consists of aggregate demand and aggregate supply functions. However, in contrast to the standard models of aggregate demand and aggregate supply, these functions are analysed not in the coordinates of a plane on the axes of which values of the price level and output are shown, but on a plane in which the vertical axis corresponds to the average tax rate t, and the horizontal axis, to output Y. In this model, the price level, together with the rest of the factors that affect aggregate demand and aggregate supply, is exogenously given.

4.1. Model of Aggregate Demand

We begin our analysis with an examination of aggregate demand functions, which we designate as $Y^D(t)$. This notation indicates that aggregate demand is considered in the form of functions of the average tax rate t. Based on a modified version of a simplified Keynesian model (see Chapter 1) it has been shown that, if analysis is limited just to the product market, then the aggregate demand function that depends on the average tax rate can be expressed in the following form:

$$Y^D(t) = \frac{\widetilde{A}}{1-(1-t)b-tg} , \qquad (4.1)$$

where $\widetilde{A}$ is planned autonomous spending; this indicator is the sum of autonomous household consumption a, autonomous government purchases $\widetilde{G}_0$,[1] gross domestic private investments I_0, and net exports NX_0:

$$\widetilde{A} = a + \widetilde{G}_0 + I_0 + NX_0 \ ;$$

b is the marginal propensity of households to consume, $0 < b < 1$; and is the marginal propensity for government purchases, $0 \le g \le 1$.

To give the aggregate demand function its final form, it is advisable to expand our analysis and, along with the product market, also look at the money market. For this purpose, we represent gross domestic investments I_0, which are a part of autonomous spending, not in the form of an exogenous quantity, but in the form of a function that depends on the interest rate (Dornbusch, & Fischer, 1990, ch. 4):

$$I_0 = \widetilde{I}_0 - \mu i \ ,$$

[1] To be more precise, $\widetilde{G}_0$ includes not the full amount of government purchases (as is customary in traditional Keynesian models), but only the part of it that does not depend on tax revenues to the national budget and is determined exogenously.

where is the part of investment spending that does not depend on the interest rate or on the amount of output (based on this content, refers to autonomous investments); is a nonnegative parameter characterizing the sensitivity of investments to the interest rate; i is the nominal interest rate. The value of i is established in the money market by the mechanism of balancing the money supply and demand. In the simplest case, the equation corresponding to equilibrium of the money market can be represented in the following form (Dornbusch, & Fischer, 1990, ch. 4):

$$\frac{M}{P} = kY^D(t) - h\,i,$$

where M/P is the real cash balance of money in circulation (it is determined by the ratio of the nominal amount of money and the price level P); and are positive coefficients expressing the sensitivity of the demand for money to aggregate spending and the interest rate i.

Taking the equations given above into account in (4.1) and making the appropriate transformations, we get the following model of aggregate demand:[2]

$$Y^D(t) = \frac{A}{1-(1-t)b - tg + \mu\,k/h}, \tag{4.2}$$

Here the quantity A consists of exogenously given elements. In particular,

$$A = a + \widetilde{G}_0 + \widetilde{I}_0 + NX_0 + \frac{\mu}{h}\left(\frac{M}{P}\right) = \widetilde{A}_0 + \frac{\mu}{h}\left(\frac{M}{P}\right). \tag{4.3}$$

As we see, in addition to the traditional autonomous spending $\widetilde{A}_0 = a + \widetilde{G}_0 + \widetilde{I}_0 + NX_0$, A also contains an element that is determined by the real cash balance of money (M/P).

---

[2] It should be noted that (4.2) differs from the well-known version of the Keynesian model of aggregate demand (from the IS–LM model) in the rule that reflects taxes and determines the aggregate $A$of autonomous elements.

It can be shown that the properties of function (4.2) are determined by the interrelation of the marginal propensity to consume b and the marginal propensity for government purchases g. All else being equal, $Y^D(t)$, in the area of its determination,[3]is increasing in relation to t when $g > b$, decreasing when $g < b$, and indifferent when $g = b$.[4]A graphic illustration of the function with various possible combinations of values of and is given in Figure 4.1. It should be noted that, all else being equal, a change in A, which is determined from (4.3), shifts the curves corresponding to $Y^D(t)$. In particular, with an increase in A, the curves shift upward in parallel, which for a given average tax rate means an increase in aggregate demand. On the other hand, with a decrease in the curves shift downward in parallel, which for a given average tax rate corresponds to a reduction in aggregate demand.

4.2. Model of Aggregate Supply

As the aggregate supply that depends on the average tax rate we can consider a function of total output that fully satisfies the conditions of the Laffer theory and has the following form (Ananiashvili, 2009):

$$Y^S(t) = Y_{pot} f(t) = Y_{pot}(-et^{\delta} \ln t^{\delta}), \tag{4.4}$$

where expresses the volume of potential output with full use of economic resources in conditions of the existing technology; is a function that reflects the institutional aspect and determines the cumulative tax effect on supply. This is a behavioral function; it shows the degree of use of existing economic resources with a given value of the average tax rate (i.e., in conditions of a given institutional environment). Based on this content, should satisfy the condition $0 \le f(t) \le 1$. When takes a value close to one, this indicates that economic activity is high for the given average tax rate and the level of use of resources is close to the maximum. The opposite situation takes place when is

[3] From the economic content of the average tax rate, it follows that $0 \le t \le 1$. These values also establish the area of determination of the function $Y^D(t)$.

[4] A detailed explanation of the reasons why aggregate demand is increasing in relation to the tax rate when $g > b$ is given in paragraph 1.3 of the Chapter 1.

close to zero. In this function, e represents the base of the natural logarithm, and is a positive parameter that we will discuss later.

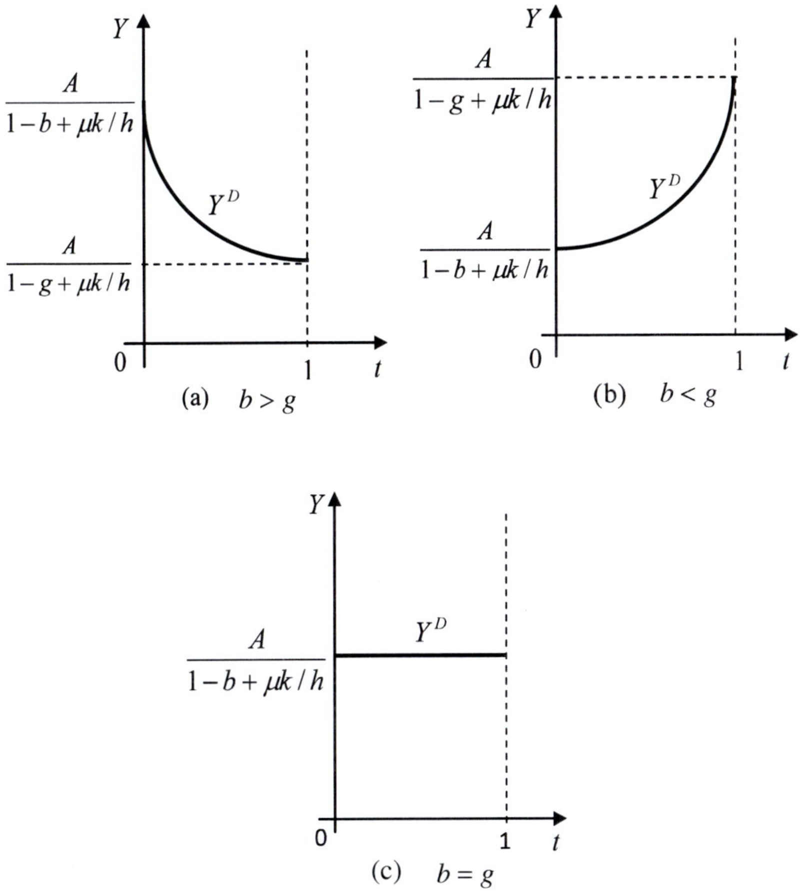

Figure 4.1.Versions of Aggregate Demand Curves.

In the Chapter 3 we have investigated the properties of the aggregate supply function (4.4) and have shown that is increasing in the interval $[0, t^*)$, decreasing in the interval $(t^*, 1]$, and

$$\lim_{t \to 0} Y^S(t) = 0, \, , t^* = \exp\left(-\tfrac{1}{\delta}\right) = e^{-1/\delta}, \; Y^S(1) = 0 .$$

With an average tax rate $t^* = e^{-1/\delta}$, the institutional environment fosters full use of resources, and output is maximum, that is, it is at the potential level Y_{pot}. Consequently, t^* can be considered *the optimal average tax rate*.

A graphic illustration of function (4.4) is given in Figure 4.2 (the curve Y^S). It shows that when all else is equal, movement on the ascending part of the curve corresponds to a change in the average tax rate from 0 to t^*; and movement on the descending part of the curve $Y^S(t)$, to a change from t^* to 1.[5]

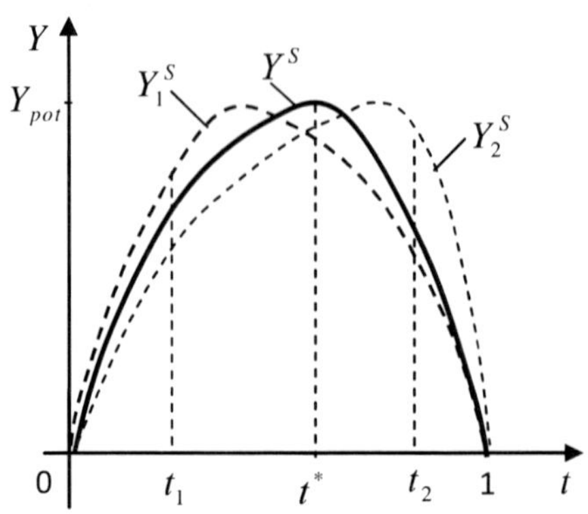

Figure 4.2. Aggregate Supply Curve and Versions of its Movement.

What happens if "all else being equal" changes?

First we should point out that in the conditions of model (4.4) for aggregate supply, a change in all else being equal involves a change either in the amount of potential output (Y_{pot}) or in the value of parameter δ.. As a rule, a change in occurs mostly in the long term, and the reason for such a change may be an increase or decrease in labor or the existing amount of capital, improvement or deterioration in the quality of technologies, a change in labor

[5] It is assumed that an increase in the tax rate is accompanied by positive and negative effects. For a value of the average tax rate in the range from 0 to t^*, the sum of the positive effects exceeds the sum of the negative ones, and therefore movement on the ascending part of the aggregate supply curve corresponds to an increase in the tax rate in this interval. The opposite relationship of positive and negative effects occurs for subsequent values of the average tax rate, and so a decrease in aggregate supply corresponds to an increase in the tax rate in the section $(t^*, 1]$. For a detailed explanation of this question, see (Ananiashvili, & Papava, 2010a).

productivity, and so on. When these changes have a positive effect on Y_{pot}, then the curve shifts upward on the coordinate plane (aggregate supply increases, i.e., with the existing average tax rate more products and services will be produced in the economy than there were before the increase in Y_{pot}). Obviously, a decrease in the amount of potential output will cause the opposite result: the curve will shift downward and, in conditions of the existing tax rate, aggregate supply will decrease. Interestingly, when all else being equal is unchanged, neither an increase nor a decrease in potential output affects the optimal value of average tax rate t^*. In other words, with a change in Y_{pot}, the maximum of function (4.4) changes, but the value of the tax rate at which this maximum is attained does not change.

A completely different situation occurs when a disruption of all else being equal in the aggregate supply model (4.4) involves a change in the current market conditions, price level, production costs per unit of output, or producers' expectations. These circumstances, especially a change in the price level, do not have affect the amount of potential output or, accordingly the maximum value of the function $Y^S(t)$; however, they do affect parameter and the optimal tax rate determined by this parameter.[6] In other words, for example, with an increase in the price level the maximum value of the function will not change; however, the value of the average tax rate at which this maximum is attained will change.[7] Consequently, in this case, a graph of the function will shift (deviate) from the position Y^S to the right or left. In Figure 4.2, the dashed curves Y_1^S and correspond to forms of the shift (deviation). The specific direction of the shift (deviation) depends on which of the intervals or the existing tax rate is in. If we assume that the tax rate is in the interval and, for example, is $t_1 \in [0, t^*)$, then with an increase in the price level, the graph of the function will shift to the position Y_1^S, while if we take as the existing rate, which is in the interval $(t^*, 1]$, that is, $t_2 \in (t^*, 1]$, then the shift

---

[6] Recall that in the aggregate supply model (4.4), t^* and parameter δ are interrelated as $t^* = e^{-1/\delta}$.

[7] The case when the economy is in a state of full employment and tax rate $t$coincides with optimal value $t^*$is an exception. In this case, an increase in the level of prices does not affect either the maximum of the function $Y^S(t)$, the parameter δ, or the tax rate t^* corresponding to it. Consequently, in this case the aggregate supply curve stays where it is.

(deviation) will be to the right, to the position Y_2^S.[8] The standard premise known from economics—that if there is not full employment, an increase in the price level (or a decrease in production costs per unit of production, or improvement of the current market conditions, etc.) has a positive effect on aggregate supply and causes it to increase—is fulfilled in the process of these changes.

4.3. Model of Macroeconomic Equilibrium

Using the aggregate demand models (4.2)–(4.3) given above and the aggregate supply model (4.4), we will write the condition of macroeconomic equilibrium $Y^S(t) = Y^D(t)$, determined in relation to the average tax rate, as follows:

$$Y_{pot}(-et^{\delta}\ln t^{\delta}) = \frac{A}{1-(1-t)b-tg+\mu k/h}. \tag{4.5}$$

Equation (4.5) is a condition of Laffer-Keynesian equilibrium. It shows that for macroeconomic equilibrium to exist, all else being equal (for the given values of autonomous spending, the real cash balance of money, and potential output), the tax rate t must be such that it satisfies equation (4.5). We will call this t the *equilibrium average tax rate.*[9] The existence of equilibrium is graphically illustrated in Figure 4.3, where represents the aggregate supply curve; and Y^D, the aggregate demand curve. In this case, Figure 4.3a corresponds to the case when in the marginal propensity for government purchases is less than the marginal propensity to consume b; Figure 4.3b, to the case when $g > b$; and Figure 4.3c, to the case when $g = b$.[10]

---

[8] It is easy to notice that when the aggregate supply curve shifts to the right, the value of the optimal tax rate decreases, and when the curve shifts to the left, it increases. Taking this into account, from the expression determining the optimal tax rate ($t^* = e^{-1/\delta}$), we will establish that a decrease in the value of parameter δ corresponds to a shift of the curve $Y^S(t)$ to the left; and an increase in δ, to a shift to the right.

[9] Based on the specifics of equation (4.5), in the general case it is not possible to derive an analytical expression for equilibrium t, but it is no problem to find it by approximate calculation methods.

[10] Recall that in the suggested version of the Keynesian model of aggregate demand, the relationship of the *b*and *g*determines the nature of the dependence of aggregate demand on

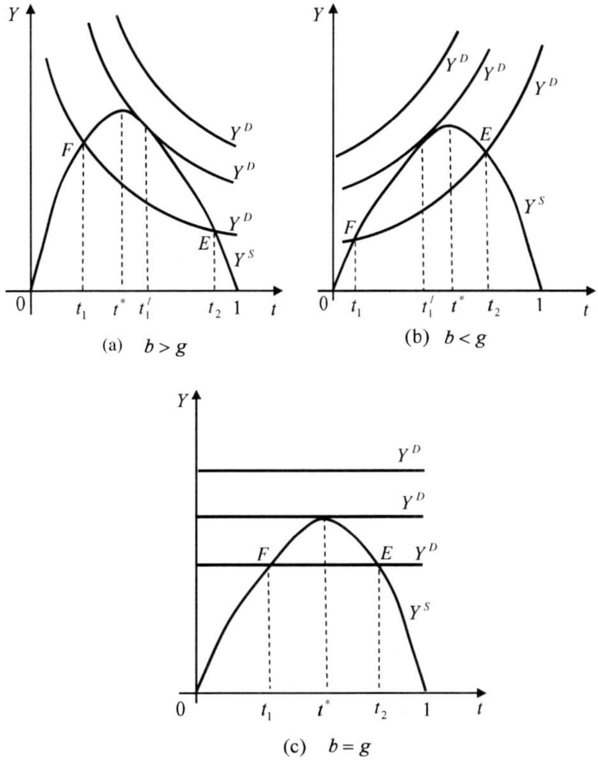

Figure 4.3. Equilibrium in Conditions of Laffer-Keynesian Synthesis.

As we see, with different relationships of and g for given values of autonomous spending $\widetilde{A}_0$, the real cash balance (M/P), and potential output Y_{pot}, three cases can take place:

1. No equilibrium average tax rate exists (the curves and Y^D do not intersect). It is clear that this happens when autonomous spending $\widetilde{A}_0$, which is part of *A*, is so large that potential output is not enough to satisfy it.
2. There are two equilibrium values of the average tax rate, t_1 and t_2 (the curves Y^S and Y^D intersect at two points), the role and values of

the average tax rate. In particular, $Y^D(t)$ decreases in relation to *t* when $b>g$, increases when $b<g$, and is indifferent when $b=g$.

which are determined by the relationship between the marginal propensity of households to consume and the marginal propensity for government purchases g. When $b > g$ (Figure 4.3a), of the two equilibrium values of the average tax rate the lower one t_1 is preferable, since it provides for greater aggregate spending; for the same reason, in the case of $b < g$ (Figure 4.3b), the higher tax rate t_2 is preferable; and finally in the case of (Figure 4.3c), both rates t_1 and provide the same result from the point of view of production, employment, and aggregate spending.

3. There is a single equilibrium tax rate (curves and Y^D touch each other at only one point). In the case of Figures 4.3a and 4.3b, this rate cannot be optimal.

Henceforth, for the sake of simplicity, of the three different relationships of and we will consider only one. In particular, we will assume that $b > g$. We pointed out above that in this situation aggregate demand is a decreasing function in relation to the average tax rate and this fully conforms to Keynesian theory. Here we note that the results for the case considered here are the same as those obtained in the other two cases.

4.4. Versions of Disruption and Restoration of Equilibrium

To clarify how equilibrium is established in conditions of the given model, we turn to equation (4.5). Since for this equation the cases of nonexistence of a solution or the existence of only one solution (the first and third of the cases indicated above) are highly unlikely, we will assume that, for the given values of A, and δ, in relation to t (4.5) has two solutions: and t_2. Consequently, for curves and Y^D given in Figure 4.4, macroeconomic equilibrium can be found at one of the points F and E. For clarity, we will assume that the starting point of economic equilibrium is F, which corresponds to the average tax rate t_1.

Suppose that, for certain reasons, the initial equilibrium is disrupted. As follows from (4.5), the reason for this could be:

- a change in aggregate demand due to a number of circumstances, including an increase or decrease in one or more of the elements of planned autonomous spending or the real cash balance;
- a purposeful change in the tax rate by the government;
- a change in aggregate supply due to an increase or decrease in potential output Y_{pot}.

We will consider each case separately.

Case 1. Restoration of Equilibrium in the Case of a Change in Aggregate Demand

We begin with the case when, all else being equal, aggregate demand undergoes a change. Specifically, we assume that it has increased thanks to an increase in some element of autonomous aggregate spending from A. This change will cause a shift of the aggregate demand curve to a new position Y_1^D (see Figure 4.4a). In the new situation that is created, as long as the tax rate is at level t_1, the amount of increased aggregate demand is determined by point and is greater than the amount of aggregate supply, which, for its part, is determined by point F. Depending on what actions the government takes, restoration of equilibrium or transition to a new equilibrium can be accomplished in two ways.

One way to establish equilibrium is to step up government activity, in particular, for it to improve tax administration and, by applying appropriate laws, to increase the value of from t_1 to t_1', in parallel with the growth of autonomous spending. Such a measure will have an effect on the amount of aggregate demand as well as aggregate supply: increasing the tax rate will reduce the amount of aggregate demand (on the aggregate demand curve it moves from point F_1 to F_2) and, according to the Laffer theory, increase the amount of aggregate supply (on the aggregate supply curve it moves from point F to F_2). As a result of these changes, a new equilibrium corresponding to the increased output is established at point F_2.

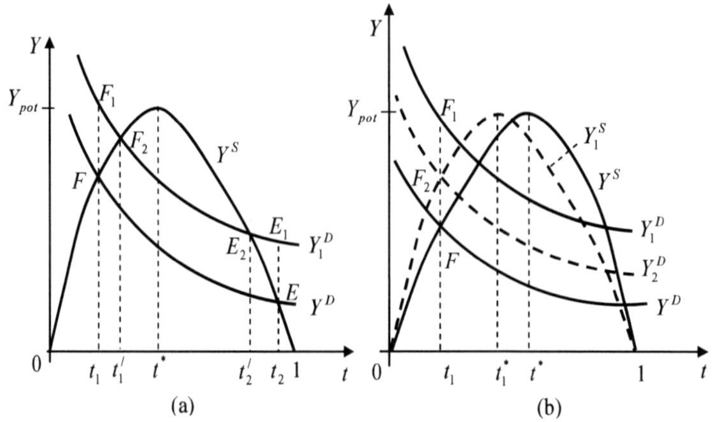

Figure 4.4. Restoration of Equilibrium in the Case of a Change in Aggregate Demand.

If the initial point of the economy's equilibrium was not at point F, but at E, the situation would be different. According to Figure 4.4a, the latter point (i.e., E) is on the descending part of the aggregate supply curve, where the negative effects of taxes play a dominant role. Therefore, if in the hypothetically created situation the government lowers the value of t from t_2 to t_2', then the economy will be able to make the transition to a new equilibrium and ensure that the increased aggregate demand is properly satisfied.

The scenario considered above for restoration of macroeconomic equilibrium is interesting from the point of view that the government, by regulating the tax rate, makes it possible to satisfy increased aggregate demand so that the price level does not change. However, if the government takes a neutral position and refrains from regulating the tax rate, then other mechanisms go to work, one of the most important of which is the market mechanism of regulation by prices.

From the standard model of aggregate demand and aggregate supply, which is analysed in coordinates of the plane of price level and total output, it follows that when the economy is in a state of less than full employment and excess demand occurs,[11] then, all else being equal, the price level rises. In the general case, this causes a decrease in aggregate demand and an increase in aggregate supply, so that equilibrium is established between them. Naturally, this mechanism also operates, with a certain specific nature, in the model

[11] We are dealing with precisely such a case.

(4.2)–(4.5) that we are examining. Its specific nature in model (4.2)–(4.5) is that in conditions of a fixed average tax rate an increase in the price level has an effect on the location of the aggregate demand and aggregate supply curves and causes them to shift.[12]The form and direction of this movement for the case when the initial macroeconomic equilibrium is at point *F*are shown in Figure 4.4b. Here, curves and express aggregate demand before the rise of the price level. In this case, Y^D is the initial curve, and is the curve that occurred after the increase in autonomous spending. Curve Y^S corresponds to the supply that existed before the change in the price level.

The aggregate demand curve, which was lowered as a result of the rise of the price level,[13]will take position Y_2^D, and the curve for the increased aggregate supply will take position Y_1^S. Consequently, the new equilibrium established as a result of the change in the price level is determined by point F_2.

We point out the circumstance that, in conditions of a fixed tax rate, a change in the price level caused by a change in autonomous spending and, accordingly, aggregate demand, has an effect on parameter δ and on the optimal tax rate determined by this parameter. When the initial equilibrium point is on the ascending part of aggregate supply (as it is in the case considered above), that is, when the tax rate $t_1$corresponding to equilibrium is less than its optimal value t^*, the growth of aggregate demand and the price level are accompanied by a process of decrease of parameter δ and movement of the optimal tax rate to the left. In this case, if the process of growth of aggregate demand continues and, consequently, the price level also continues to rise, a time will come when the optimal tax rate becomes equal to the given fixed value of $t_1$corresponding to equilibrium.

The opposite situation takes place when the initial equilibrium point is on the descending part of curve Y^S and the tax rate corresponding to equilibrium is greater than its optimal value t^*. In these conditions, with a fixed value of the tax rate, growth of aggregate demand and, accordingly, the price level causes growth in parameter δ, a shift of the aggregate supply curve to the left, and

[12] A change in the price level within the limits of model (4.2)–(4.5) means a disruption of "all else being equal." Therefore, on the coordinate plane of the tax rate and output a change in the price level has an effect on the location of the curves Y^D and Y^S, while in the standard model of aggregate demand and aggregate supply, a change in the price level causes movement on the curves Y^D and Y^S.

[13] The point is that when *P*rises, all else being equal, *A*decreases, since the latter includes the element *M*/*P*, which depends on *P*(see equation (4.3)).

movement of the optimal tax rate toward the rate corresponding to equilibrium. In this case, if aggregate demand increases to a certain level, then the tax rate corresponding to the initial equilibrium will become the optimal rate.

The main conclusion from analyzing the version of restoration of equilibrium considered above is that with a change in parameter δ caused by a change in the price level, the equilibrium and optimal values of the tax rate come closer together.

Case 2. Restoration of Equilibrium in the Case of a Change in the Tax Rate

We consider the case when the reason for disruption of equilibrium F is a purposeful change in the tax rate t_1 by the government. As in the previous case, we will assume that the average tax rate t_1(see Figure 4.5a), which is less than the fiscal Laffer point of the first kind t^*, corresponds to the initial equilibrium. Suppose that the government has decided to switch to optimal taxation t^* and has raised the average tax rate accordingly. All else being equal, according to the Laffer theory, because of the dominance of positive effects, transition to the new tax regime t^* will cause a growth in aggregate supply, which will be reflected accordingly on curve Y^S: there will be a transition from point F to point F_2. At the same time, the increased tax rate will have an effect on aggregate demand, and movement from point F to point F_1 will begin on curve Y^D. Consequently, as we can see from Figure 4.5a, an increase in the tax rate in some period will lead to the appearance of excess supply. In the situation that has been created, there are two possible ways of restoring equilibrium.

In one of them, in parallel with increased taxes, the government should promote growth of aggregate demand, for example, by making additional autonomous purchases or conducting an expansionary monetary policy. This will be a logical continuation of the actions that it has begun. If the government can increase the aggregate A(which consists of elements of autonomous spending and the real cash balance) to the level[14] $A = Y_{pot}[(1-b) + t^*(b-g) + \mu\, k/h]$ in this way and the aggregate demand curve is shifted to position Y_1^D, then equilibrium is restored, with output

[14] This formula is directly derived from (4.5) by substituting t^* into it and taking into account that $f(t^*) = -e(t^*)^{\delta} \ln(t^*)^{\delta} = 1$.

reaching its potential value, so that the price level will not change (Figure 4.5a)

From the version of establishing equilibrium considered here, it follows that just putting the optimal tax rate into effect cannot ensure employment growth and initiate the transition to equilibrium corresponding to potential output. In conditions of a Laffer-Keynesian synthesis, along with the tax regime, aggregate demand plays a significant role in achieving increased economic activity and full employment.

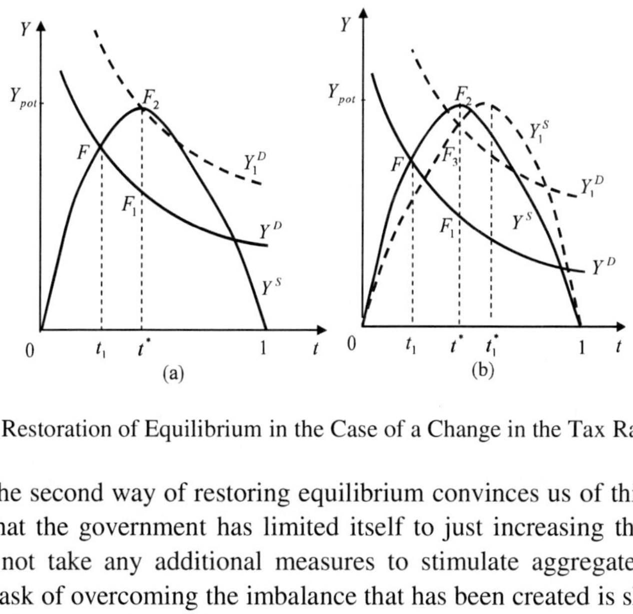

Figure 4.5. Restoration of Equilibrium in the Case of a Change in the Tax Rate.

And the second way of restoring equilibrium convinces us of this. In fact, suppose that the government has limited itself to just increasing the tax rate and does not take any additional measures to stimulate aggregate demand. Then the task of overcoming the imbalance that has been created is shouldered by the economy's main market mechanism: the price regulation mechanism. The point is that excess aggregate supply stimulates a reduction in the price level. In this process, aggregate demand begins to grow, and its curve shifts upward, from position to position Y_1^D, while aggregate supply decreases, and its curve shifts from position to the right, to position (Figure 4.5b).[15] Ultimately, a new equilibrium will appear at point F_3 instead of F_2, and it will correspond to less than the potential output. Moreover, rate t^* will lose the function of optimality, and in the situation that has been created the role of

[15] We pointed out above that in model (4.2)–(4.5) a change in the price level affects the position of the aggregate demand and aggregate supply curves.

the optimal tax rate will be assigned to t_1^*. Consequently, the government's attempt to create full employment in the economy exclusively by adjusting the tax rate will not be successful if it is not assisted by appropriate aggregate demand.

Case 3. Restoration of Equilibrium in the Case of a Change in Aggregate Supply

Another cause of disruption of equilibrium could be a change in factors determining the level of potential output, for example, an increase or decrease in the existing amount of labor or capital, or deterioration or improvement in the level of technology. In all of these cases, Y_{pot}, which is part of the aggregate supply function, undergoes a change and, because of this, aggregate supply also changes. Geometrically, this circumstance is expressed in a shift of aggregate supply curve Y^S, except that, in contrast to the movements considered previously, in this case shifts upward if increases, and downward if decreases.

Suppose that, in conditions of initial equilibrium F, the value of potential output was Y_{pot}, and the aggregate supply corresponding to it was described by curve Y^S (Figure 4.6). Say that the value of has increased to Y_{pot}^1 because of an improvement in technology. All else being equal, this will cause a shift of the aggregate supply curve to position and a temporary disruption of equilibrium: for the existing tax rate t_1, output will reach point F_1, provided that aggregate demand is determined by point F. A situation of excess aggregate supply is created, and there are three ways to bring it back into equilibrium:

1. To reduce the amount of aggregate supply and stimulate aggregate demand, the government should lower the existing average tax rate in the case of Figure 4.6a, and increase it to point t_2 in the case of Figure 4.6b. As a result of these actions, a new equilibrium is created at point F_3, which corresponds to higher equilibrium output in Figure 4.6a and lower equilibrium output in Figure 4.6b.
2. In conditions of the existing tax rate, by means of fiscal and monetary policy, the government should encourage an increase in aggregate

demand to a level such that curve Y^D shifts to point F_1. If this happens, then the new equilibrium will be at point F_1.[16]

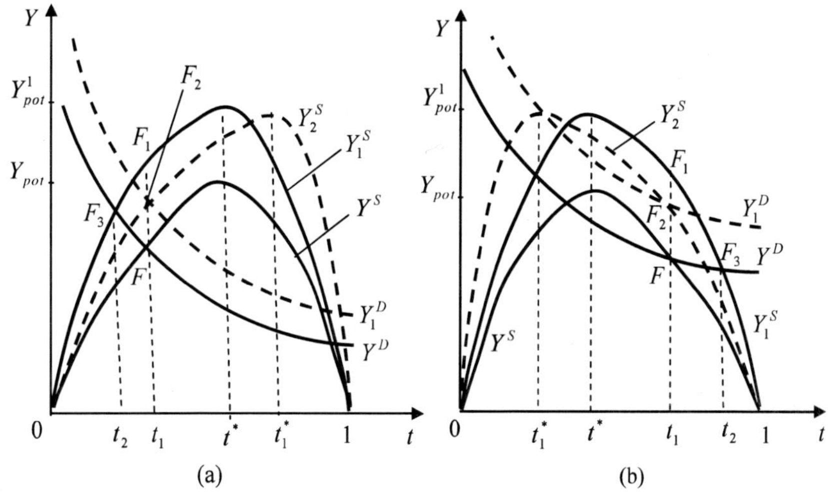

Figure 4.6. Effect of a Change in Potential Output on the Equilibrium Position.

3. If the government does not intervene in the process of creating equilibrium, then, because of the excess demand, the mechanism of self-regulation will take effect, and the price level will decline. On the one hand, this will increase aggregate demand, and the aggregate demand curve will shift to position Y_1^D; on the other hand, it will decrease aggregate supply and shift the aggregate supply curve from position to Y_2^S. In the end, a new equilibrium position will be created at point F_2, at which the level of output and employment are higher than at the initial equilibrium point F.

We will call attention to the circumstance that, even in this case, a change in the price level causes a shift of the aggregate supply curve, and this is once again followed by a change in the optimal tax rate, which shifts from point t^*

[16] The distinctive feature of these two ways of establishing a new equilibrium is that the government, by conducting a well-thought-out economic policy, makes it possible to increase the level of employment and production so that the price level stays at the point where it was in conditions of the initial equilibrium.

to t_1^*. Hence the conclusion can be drawn that when the government keeps the average tax rate in a stable position, then each new equilibrium price level has its own optimal tax rate.

4.5. THE FAMILY OF LAFFER CURVES

Analysis of model (4.2)–(4.5) of Laffer-Keynesian equilibrium has shown that when the tax rate is fixed, changes that occur in the economy have an effect on the aggregate supply function (4.4) and cause a change in parameter δ. This means that each given value of the equilibrium tax rate can correspond to a whole set of aggregate supply functions and, accordingly, supply curves that differ from each other in the value of parameter δ (or in the value of the optimal tax rate t^*, which is the same thing). Because of this, aggregate supply Y^S can be seen as a function of two variables, t and δ:

$$Y^S = Y^S(t, \delta).$$

In this notation, all else being equal, t reflects the weight of the tax burden. As for δ, to explain its content we have to take into account the circumstance that the aggregate supply model (4.4) is, in essence, a behavioral model expressing the result of economic agents' expected response in conditions of a tax burden of one weight or another. Naturally, in various situations existing in the economy, this response may not be the same for the same tax burden, the more so as the behavior and decision making of most economic agents is based on rationalism. And the latter, as we know, implies that economic agents optimize their behavior not just once, but over and over, continuously, taking each new circumstance into account. Consequently, parameter δ quantitatively expresses the result of the circumstances that may have an effect on the nature of the relationship that exists between aggregate supply and the tax burden.[17]

Like the aggregate supply function, the version of the budget revenues function determined on the basis of the supply function, that is, the Laffer

[17] As we pointed out above, among these circumstances a special role is played by a change in the price level, therefore, instead of δ we can use the notation $\delta = \delta(P)$, and the notation of the aggregate supply function $Y^S(t)$ can be replaced by $Y^S = Y^S(t, \delta(P))$.

function, should be seen as a function of two variables. In the conditions of model (4.2)–(4.5) under consideration here, it has the following form:

$$T^S(t) = tY^S(t) = Y_{pot}(-et^{\delta+1}\ln t^{\delta}), \tag{4.6}$$

where $T^S(t)$ is the amount of the budget's tax revenues with a tax base $Y^S(t)$. Consequently, we can write:

$$T^S = tY^S(t,\delta) = T^S(t,\delta).$$

It can be shown that tax rate t^{**} corresponding to the maximum of the Laffer function (4.6), which is also called the Laffer point of the second kind,is determined as follows (Ananiashvili and Papava, 2010a):

$$t^{**} = \exp\left(-\frac{1}{(1+\delta)}\right).$$

From this expression, it follows that with a change in δ, the value of t^{**} also changes, and, like the supply curves, a set, or family, of Laffer curves is obtained.[18] However, in contrast to the aggregate supply curve, which has the same value of the maximum for all δ, the maximum value of the Laffer curve (4.6) is different for various δ. The point is that for function (4.6), the following condition takes place:

$$\max_t T^S(t,\delta) = \frac{\delta}{1+\delta} Y_{pot}.$$

Therefore, with a change in δ, the value of the tax rate corresponding to the maximum of the Laffer curve changes, as does the maximum amount of tax revenues that can be obtained with that tax rate. In particular, increases with an increase in and decreases with a decrease. Consequently, a shift of t^{**} to the right on the tax rate axis is accompanied by an increase in $T^S(t^{**},\delta)$.

---

[18] It should be noted that there are now many articles and studies confirming or refuting the concept of the Laffer curve and problems of its practical realization (see, Chapter 2), all of them unequivocally analyse a single curve, rather than a set of curves.

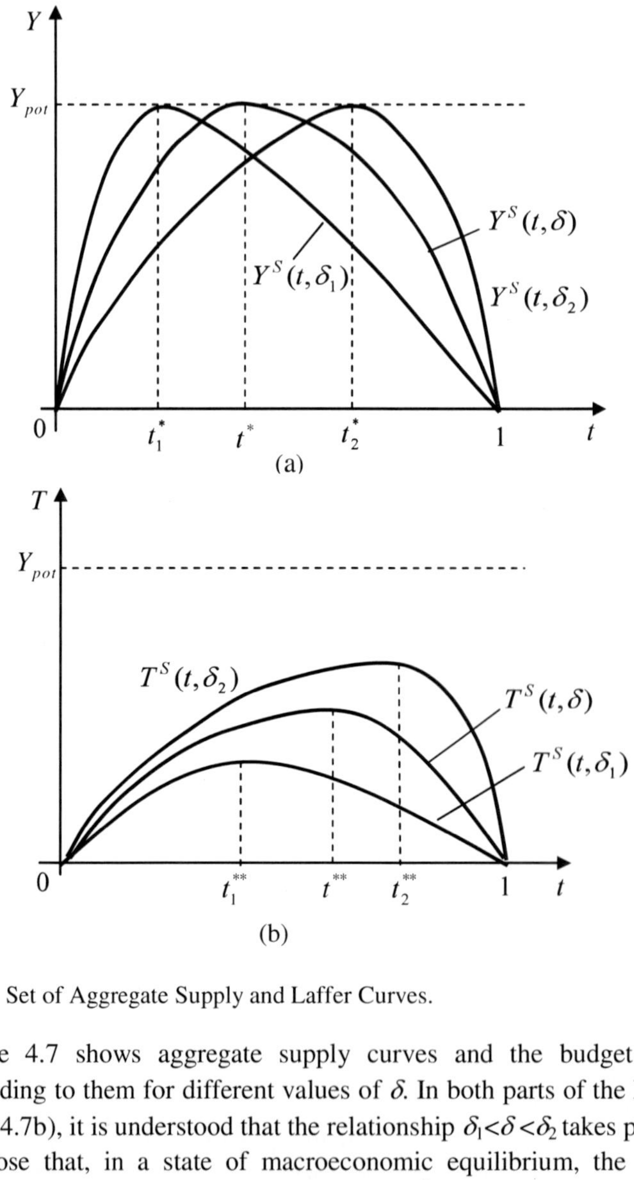

Figure 4.7. Set of Aggregate Supply and Laffer Curves.

Figure 4.7 shows aggregate supply curves and the budget revenues corresponding to them for different values of δ. In both parts of the Figure 4.7 (4.7a and 4.7b), it is understood that the relationship $\delta_1 < \delta < \delta_2$ takes place.

Suppose that, in a state of macroeconomic equilibrium, the aggregate supply curve corresponding to the given rate t is Y^S (t, δ), and the Laffer curve is T^S (t, δ) (see Figure 4.7). Say that, in these conditions, aggregate demand has increased, and the government has decided to keep the tax rate at the existing level t. We already know that when the initial macroeconomic equilibrium is on the ascending part of the supply curve Y^S (t, δ), then in the newly created situation, new aggregate supply Y^S (t, δ_1) and Laffer functions and curves T^S (t, δ_1) will be formed, and the δ_1 corresponding to these curves is less than δ. If we assume that, in the same situation, the initial macroeconomic equilibrium is on the descending part of the supply curve Y^S (t, δ), then the new aggregate supply and Laffer functions and curves take the form determined by Y^S (t, δ_2) and T^S (t, δ_2), respectively. It is clear that opposite changes will occur in the case of a decrease in aggregate demand: the aggregate supply and Laffer curves will shift to positions Y^S (t, δ_2) and Y^S (t, δ_2), respectively, if the initial macroeconomic equilibrium is on the ascending part of the initial equilibrium, and to the positions Y^S (t, δ_1) and T^S (t, δ_1), if it is on the descending part.

From the analysis that has been done, it follows that the Laffer curve is not a stable construct and can change depending on the situation that has been created in the economy, especially as a result of a change in the price level, which also implies a change in t^{**}. In such conditions, the widespread opinion among proponents of the theory that it is desirable to somehow determine the value of the tax rate t^{**} that provides maximum tax revenues to the national budget, which is the basis for developing economic policy and improving the existing tax regime, loses its attractiveness, since, because of the changes occurring in the economy, it will be necessary to change the established rate and in the final analysis this will produce an undesirable result.[19]

[19] In the opinion of the well-known economist Robert Barro, constant changes in the tax rate (either increases or decreases) cause greater distortions and irrecoverable losses than a tax regime that has a fixed rate (see, e.g., Barro, 1979; Sachs, & Larrain, 1993, Ch. 7).

CONCLUSION

Based on an analysis of a modified version of the standard Keynesian model of a product market, it is shown that a change in the average tax rate has a complex effect on aggregate demand. Depending on the marginal propensity of households to consume and the marginal propensity for government purchases, an increase in the average tax rate may lead to either a decrease or an increase in aggregate demand. In this case, since the parameter of marginal propensities to purchase is easily regulated, by selecting its appropriate value the government can purposefully use a tax increase to stimulate or to reduce aggregate demand.

The Laffer Curve is the most evident illustration of the key postulations of the supply-side economics. Presently, almost all modern economics textbooks are evidently critical of the Laffer Curve. Despite this, there are a number of most recent works aimed at studying mathematical and empirical implications of the Laffer Curve. It must be underlined that originally the Laffer Curve was formulated in a macroeconomic context, for which reason it is not applicable to individual taxes, but rather to a certain average aggregate tax.

The modifications to the Laffer Curve are based on a factor of time. High importance is the question—in which direction the average aggregate tax is changing: upward or downward, when the Laffer Effect always appears a couple of years later.

There are two different approaches to estimating the effect of the tax burden on the amount of total output and budget revenues. The first approach is based on a transformation model, in which the main role is played by a production function with variable elasticity. The second approach uses a behavioral model, with a specific version of an entropy function. Both models make it possible to determine the so-called fiscal points corresponding to the maximum production effect and the budget's maximum tax revenues. The conclusion is drawn that, of these points, only the points of the behavioral model correspond to the Laffer concept, since for points derived from the transformation model the amount of use of economic resources is exogenous, while for the points of the behavioral model this amount occurs endogenously. The results obtained are illustrated using existing data on the U.S. economy.

The combining of the Laffer Curve approach with the Keynesian approach cutting of taxes, leads to a form of Laffer-Keynesian synthesis.

The Laffer-Keynesian synthesis based on a macroeconomic equilibrium model in which aggregate demand and aggregate supply are considered not in relation to the price level, as is traditionally done, but in terms of functions dependent on the average tax rate. The concepts of optimal and equilibrium tax rates are introduced. In the former case, aggregate supply is maximum, while in the latter case aggregate demand and supply coincide. Based on an analysis of the model, it is shown that when the government tries to maintain the equilibrium average tax rate at a fixed level, the optimal tax rate becomes dependent on the price level, and an appropriate change in aggregate demand may lead to approximation of the optimal rate to the equilibrium rate. It is also demonstrated that each given value of the equilibrium tax rate can be matched with a set of functions and curves of aggregate supply and the national budget's tax revenues.

References

Aleksashenko, S. V., Kiselev, D. A. Teplukhin, P. M. & Yasin, E. G. (1989). "Nalogovye shkaly: funktsii, svoistva, metodi upravlenia" [Tax Scales: Functions, Properties and Management Methods]. *Ekonomika i matematiceskie metody* [Economics and Mathematical Methods], Vol. *25*, No. 3.(In Russian.)

Ananiashvili, I. (2008). "gadasakhadebis zegavlena ertobliv motkhovnaze" [Taxe Impact on the Aggregate Demand]. *Ekonomika da biznesi* [Economics and Business], No. 3.(In Georgian.)

Ananiashvili, I. (2009). "gadasakhadebis zegavlena ertobliv mitsodebaze" [Taxe Impact on the Aggregate Supply]. *Ekonomika da biznesi* [Economics and Business], No. 1.(In Georgian.)

Ananiashvili, I. (2010). "saqartvelos ekonomikis potentsiuri mtliani shida produqtisa da umushevrobis bunebrivi donis ekonometrikuli shephaseba" [Econometric Evaluation of the Potential Gross Domestic Product and the Natural Rate of Unemployment of Georgia's Economy]. *Ekonomika da biznesi* [Economics and Business], No. 5.(In Georgian.)

Ananiashvili, I. & Papava.V. (2009). *gadasakhadebi, motkhovna da mitsodeba: lapher-keinzianuri sintezi* [Taxes, Demand and Supply: Laffer-Keynesian Synthesis]. Tbilisi: Siakhle. (In Georgian.)

Ananiashvili, I. & Papava.V. (2010a). "Modeli otsenki vlianiia nalogov na rezul'taty ekonomicheskoi deiatel'nosti" [Factor Score Models of Taxes on the Results of Economic Activity]. *Ekonomika, Finansy, Nalogi* [Economy, Finances, Taxes], No. 2.(In Russian.)

Ananiashvili, I. & Papava, V. (2010b). *Nalogi i makroekonomicheskoe ravnovesie: Laffero-keinsianskii' sintez* [Taxes and Macroeconomic

Equilibrium: Laffer-Keynesian Synthesis]. Stockholm: CA&CC Press. (In Russian.)

Ananiashvili, I. & Papava, V. (2012a). "Macroeconomic Model of Laffer-Keynesian Synthesis." *Problems of Economic Transition*, Vol. *54*, No. 12.

Ananiashvili, I. & Papava, V. (2012b). "Taxes, Production Technology, and Economic Growth." *Problems of Economic Transition*, Vol. *54*, No. 12.

Ananiashvili, I. & Papava, V. (2012c). "The Role of the Average Tax Rate in the Keynesian Model of Aggregate Demand." *Problems of Economic Transition*, Vol. *54*, No. 12.

Arkin, V., Slastnikov, A. & Shevtsova, E. (1999). *Nalogovoe stimulirovanie investitsionnykh protsessov* [Tax Stimulation of Investment Processes]. Moscow: RPEI/Eurasian Foundation. (In Russian.)

Atkinson, A. B. & Stiglitz, J. E. (1980). *Lectures on Public Economics*. New York: McGraw-Hill McGraw-Hill Publishing Company.

Balatsky, E. V. (1997a). "Fiskalnoe regulirovanie v inflatsionnoi srede" [Fiscal Regulation in an Inflationary Environment]. *Mirovaia ekonomika i mezhdunarodnye otnosheniia* [World Economy and International Relations],No. 1.(In Russian.)

Balatsky, E. V. (1997b). "Lafferovy effecty i finansovye kriterii ekonomicheskoi deiatel'nosti" [Laffer Effects and Financial Criteria of Economic Activity]. *Mirovaia ekonomika i mezhdunarodnye otnosheniia* [World Economy and International Relations], No. 11.(In Russian.)

Balatsky, E. V. (1997c). "Tochki Laffera i ikh kolichestvennaia otsenka" [Laffer Points and Quantitative Assessment of Them]. *Mirovaia ekonomika i mezhdunarodnye otnosheniia* [World Economy and International Relations], No. 12.(In Russian.)

Balatsky, E. V. (1999). "Nalog na imushchestvo firm i nakoplenie osnovnogo kapitala" [Corporate Property Tax and Accumulation of Fixed Assets].*Mirovaia ekonomika i mezhdunarodnye otnosheniia* [World Economy and International Relations], No. 3. (In Russian.)

Balatsky, E. V. (2000a). "Effektivnost' fiskal'noi politiki gosudarstva" [Effectiveness of Government the Fiscal Policy]. *Problemy prognozirovanija* [Problems of Forecasting], No. 5.(In Russian.)

Balatsky, E. V. (2000b). "Otsenka ob"ema potentsial'nogo VVP" [Estimation of the GDP's Potential Volume]. *Problemy prognozirovaniia* [Problems of Forecasting], No. 1. (In Russian.)

Balatsky, E. V. (2000c). "Vosproizvodstvennyi tsikl i nalogovoe bremia" [The Reproduction Cycle and the Tax Burden]. *Ekonomika i matematicheskie metody* [Economics and Mathematical Methods], Vol. *36*, No. 1. (In Russian.)

Balatsky, E. V. (2003). "Analiz vliianiia nalogovoi nagruzki na ekonomicheskii rost s pomosch'iu proizvodstvenno-institutsional'nykh funktsii" [Impact Analysis of the Tax Burden on the Economic Growth with Production- Institutional Functions]. *Problemy prognozirovaniia* [Problems of Forecasting], No. 2. (In Russian.)

Balatsky, E. V. (2004). "Otsenka vliianiia fiskal'nykh instrumentov na ekonomicheskii rost" [Factor Score of the Fiscal Instruments on the Economic Growth]. *Problemy prognozirovaniia* [Problems of Forecasting], No. 4. (In Russian.)

Balatsky, E. V. (2011). "Invariantnost' fiskal'nykh tochek Laffera" [Invariance of the Laffer Fiscal Points]. *Kapital strany* [Capital of the Country], August 28, *on-line at* http://www.kapital-rus.ru/index.php/articles/article/190047. (In Russian.)

Balatsky, E. & Ekimova, N. (2012). "Fiscal Policy and Economic Growth."*Problems of Economic Transition*, Vol. *54*, No. 12.

Balatsky, E. V. (2012). "Wagner's Law, the Armey-Rahn Curve, and Paradox of Wealth ." *Problems of Economic Transition*, Vol. *54*, No. 12.

Barro, R. (1979). "On the Determination of Public Debt." *Jurnal of Public Economy*, Vol. *87*, Iss. 5, Part 1.

Becker, G. S. (1998). "A Free-Market Winner vs. a Soviet-Style Loser."*Business Week*, Iss. 3589, August 3, *on-line at* http://home.uchicago.
edu/gbecker/Businessweek/BW/1998/08_03_1998.pdf.

Blanchard, O. (2009). *Macroeconomics*. Upper Saddle River, N.J.: Prentice Hall.

Bobrova, A. (2005). "O kriterii optimal'nogo nalogovogo bremeni" [On the Criterion of the Optimal Tax Burden]. *Obshchestvo i ekonomiki* [Society and Economics], No. 10–11. (In Russian.)

Bukach, B. A. (2011). "Analiz osnovnykh dopushchenii' krivoi' Laffere" [Analysis of the Main Presumption of the Laffer Curve]. *Vestnik Sevastopol'skogo natsional'nogo universiteta* [Bulletin of the Sevastopol National University], No. 116. (In Russian.)

Canto, V. A., Joiness, D. H. & Laffer, A. B. (1983). *Foundations of Supply-Side Economics: Theory and Evidence*. New York: Academic Press.

Corrado, C. & Mattey, J. (1997). "Capacity Utilization." *Journal of Economic Perspectives*, Vol. *11*, No. 1.

Dagaev, A. A. (1995). "Investitsii i nalogovaia politika (kontury obnovliaiushei'sya paradigmy)" [Investments and Tax Policy (Outlines of a Reviving Paradigm)].*Ekonomist* [Economist], No. 10. (In Russian.)

Dagaev, A. A. (2001). "Privediot li snizhenie nalogov k uvelicheniu investitsii?" [Will a Tax Cut Lead to Increased Investment?]. *Mirovaja ekonomika i mezdunarodnye otnosenija* [World Economy and International Relations], No. 1. (In Russian.)

Document, (2009). *President Ronald Reagan's Initial Actions Project.* With special Introduction by Arthur D. Laffer. New York: Threshold Editions.

Dornbusch, R. & Fischer, S. (1990). *Macroeconomics.* New York: McGraw-Hill Publishing Company.

Emery, M. E. & Chang, C. P. (1997). "Is There a Stable Relationship Between Capacity Utilization and Inflation?" *Economic Review*, Federal Reserve Bank of Dallas, First Quarter.

Gandhi, V. P., Ebrill, L. P., Mackenzie, G. A. & others. (1987). *Supply-Side Tax Policy. It's Relevance to Developing Countries.* Washington, D.C.: IMF.

Garner, A. C. (1994). "Capacity Utilization & U.S. Inflation." *Economic Review*, Federal Reserve Bank of Kansas City, Vol. *74*, No. 4.

Guesnerie, R. (1998). *A Contribution to the Pure Theory of Taxation.* Cambridge: Cambridge University Press.

Gusakov, S. V. & Zhak, S. V. (1995). "Optimal'nye ravnovesnye tseny i tochka Laffera" [Optimum Equilibrium Prices and the Laffer Point]. *Ekonomika i matematiceskie metody* [Economics and Mathematical Methods], Vol. *31*, No. 4.

Herr, H. & Kazandziska, M. (2011). *Macroeconomic Policy Regimes in Western Industrial Countries.* Oxon: Routledge.

IMF, (2005).*Russian Federation: Selected Issues.* IMF Country Report No. 05/379, October, *on-line at* http://www.imf.org/external/pubs/ft/scr/2005/cr05379.pdf.

Johansen, L. (1978). *Lectures on Macroeconomic Planning.Part 1 : General Aspects.* Amsterdam: North-Holland Publishing Company.

Kapitonenko, V. V. (1994). "Inflatsionnyi sdvig nalogovoi stavki na krivoi Laffera" [Inflation Shift of the Tax Rate on the Laffer Curve]. In *Ekonomika i tekhnologija* [The Economy and Technology]. Moscow: REA. (In Russian.)

Kleiner, G. B. (1986). *Proizvodstvennye Funktsii: Teoriia, metody, primenenie* [Production Functions: Theory, Methods, Application]. Moscow: Finansy i statistika. (In Russian.)

Knotek, II, E. S. (2007). "How Useful is Okun's Law?" *Economic Review*, Federal Reserve Bank of Kansas City, Fourth Quarter.

Kochetov, N. (2006). "Ob otsenke nalogovoi nagruzki na finansovye potoki predpriiatii" [On the Estimation of the Tax Burden on the Flow of Funds of the Enterprise]. *Obshchestvo i ekonomika* [Society and Economics], No. 9. (In Russian.)

Kolosnitsina, M. G. (2003). "Ekonomika obshchestvennogo sektora: gosudarstvennye raskhody" [Public Sector Economics: Government Spending]. *Ekonomicheskii' zhurnal Vyshei' Shkoly Ekonomiki* [*Economic Journal of the High School of Economics*], No. 3. (In Russian.)

Krugman, P. (1994). *Peddling Prosperity: Economic Sense and Nonsense in the Age of Diminished Expectations*. New York: Norton.

Krugman, P. (1998). *The Accidental Theorist: and Other Dispatches from the Dismal Science*. New York: Norton.

Laffer, A. (2004). "The Laffer Curve: Past, Present, & Future." *The Heritage Foundation, June 1, on-line at* http://www.heritage.org/research/reports/2004/06/the-laffer-curve-past-present-and-future.

Laffer, A. D., Hass, W. J. & Pryor IV, S. G. (2009). *The Private Equity Edge: How Private Equity Players and the World's Top Companies Build Value and Wealth*. New York: The McGraw-Hill Companies.

Laffer, A. D. & Moore, S. (2010). *Return to Prosperity: How America Cab Regain its Economic Superpower Status*. New York: Threshold Editions.

Laffer, A. D., Moore, S. & Tanous, P. J. (2008). *The End of Prosperity: How Higher Taxes will Doom the Economy*. New York: Threshold Editions.

Langdana, F. K. (2010). *Macroeconomic Policy.Demystifying Monetary and Fiscal Policy*. New York: Springer.

Lee, J. (2000). "The Robustness of Okun's Law: Evidence from OECD Countries." *Journal of Macroeconomics*, Vol. *22*, No. 2.

Leibfritz, W., Thornton, J. & Bibbee, A. (1997). *Taxation and Economic Performance*.OECD Economic Department Working Papers, No. 176.

Loladze, G. O. (2002). "lapheris mrudis zogierti aspeqtis shesakheb" [On the Some Aspects of the Laffer Curve]. *mikro-makro ekonomika* [micro-macroeconomics], 2002, No. 9. (In Georgian.)

Mankiw, N. G. (1992). *Macroeconomics*. New York: Worth Publishers.

Mankiw, N. G. (2004). *Principles of Economics*. Mason, OH.: South-Western.

Matthiessen, L. (1966). "A Note on the Haavelmo Theorem."*The Swedish Journal of Economics,*Vol. *68*, No. 4.

McConnell, C. R. & Brue, S. L. (2008). *Economics: Principles, Problems, and Policies*. New York: McGraw-Hill/Irwin.

McElhattan, R. (1985). "Inflation, Supply Shocks, and the Stable Inflation Rate of Capacity Utilization." *Economic Review*, Federal Reserve Bank of San Francisco, Winter.

Merkulova, T. V. (2007). "Snizhenie nalogovoi' nagruzki i effekt Laffera: argumenty i zabluzhdenia" [Reduction of the Tax Burden and Laffer Effect: Arguments and Delusions]. In *Nalogooblozhenie: problemy nauki i praktiki* [Taxation: Problems of the Science and Practice]. Khar'kov: ID "INZHEK." (In Russian.)

Mishkin, F. S. (2007). *Estimating Potential Output.* Conference on Price Measurement for Monetary Policy, Federal Reserve Bank of Dallas, Dallas, Texas, May 24, 2007, on-line at www.federalreserve.gov/newsevents/speech/mishkin20070524a.htm.

Moustapha, A. F. (1992). "Supply-Oriented Adjustment Policies." In *Macroeconomic Adjustment: Policy Instruments and Issues*, J. M. Davis, ed. Washington, D.C.: IMF.

Movshovich, S. & Sokolovski, L. (1994). "Vypusk, nalogi i krivaia Laffera" [Output, Taxes, and the Laffer Curve]. *Ekonomika i matematiceskie metody* [Economics and Mathematical Methods], Vol. *30*, No. 3. (In Russian.)

Naumov, A. A. (1998). "Biudzhetnaia politika SShA v 80–90 gody" [U.S. Budget Policy in the 1980–90s]. *Mirovaia ekonomika i mezhdunarodnye otnosheniia* [World Economy and International Relations], No. 12. (In Russian.)

Naumov, A. A. (1999). "Biudzhetnaia politika SShA v kontse stoletia" [U.S. Budget Policy at the End of the Century]. *SShA. Kanada. Ekonomika, politika, kul'tura* [USA. Canada. EConomy, Politics, Culture], No. 12. (In Russian.)

Okun, A. M. (1962). "Potential G.N.P.: Its Measurement and Significance." *Proceedings of the Business and Economic Statistics Section of American Statistical Association.*

Okun, A. M. (1970). "Potential GNP: Its Measurement and Significance." In *The Political Economy of Prosperity*. New York: Norton.

Padovano, F. & Galli, E. (2001). "Tax Rates and Economic Growth in the OECD Countries (1950–1990)." *Economic Inquiry*, Vol. *39*, No. 1.

Papava, V. (1996). "The Georgian Economy: From 'Shock Therapy' to 'Social Promotion'." *Communist Economies & Economic Transformation*, Vol. *8*, No. 2.

Papava, V. (1999). "The Georgian Economy: Main Directions and Initial Results of Reforms." In *Systemic Change in Post-Communist Economies.*

Selected Papers from the Fifth World Congress of Central and East European Studies, Warsaw, 1995, P. G. Hare, ed. London: Macmillan Press.

Papava, V. (2002a). "Necroeconomics—the Theory of Post-Communist Transformation of an Economy."*International Journal of Social Economics*, 2002, Vol. *29*, No. 9-10.

Papava, V. (2002b). "On the Laffer Effect in Post-Communist Economies (On the Bases of the Observation of Russian Literature)."*Problems of Economic Transition*, Vol. *45*, No. 7.

Papava, V. (2003). *Splendours and Miseries of the IMF in Post-Communist Georgia*.Laredo, we-publish.com.

Papava, V. (2005). *Necroeconomics.The Political Economy of Post-Communist Capitalism*. New York: iUniverse.

Papava, V. (2008). "Theoretical Foundations of the Laffer Curve." *Bulletin of the Georgian National Academy of Sciences*, Vol. *2*, No. 1.

Papava, V. (2009). "Alternatives of the Laffer Curve with 'Hysteresis'." *Bulletin of the Georgian National Academy of Sciences*, Vol. *3*, No. 1.

Puljic, M. (2006). *The Application of the Laffer Curve Approach in the Problem of Indebtedness*. Seminar Paper, Vertiefungskurs VI—SBWL Außenhandel, Vienna—12 December. Vienna: Wirtschaftsuniversität Wien, Institut für BWL des Außenhandels, Europainstitut.

Passell, P. (1996). "A Big Tax Cut to Lift the Economy. Not here, in Ukraine." *The New York Times*, November 14, *on-line at* http://www.nytimes.com/1996/11/14/business/a-big-tax-cut-to-lift-the-economy-not-here-in-ukraine.html.

Raiatskas, R. L. & Plakunov, M. K. (1987). *Kolichestvennyi analiz v ekonomiki* [Quantitative Analysis in Economics]. Moscow: Nauka. (In Russian.)

Roubini, N. (1997). *Supply Side Economics: Do Tax Rate Cuts Increase Growth and Revenues and Reduce Budget Deficits ? Or Is It Voodoo Economics All Over Again?*. Stern School of Business, New York University, *on-line at* http://people.stern.nyu.edu/nroubini/SUPPLY.HTM#act2.

Sachs, J. D. & Larrain, F. B. (1993). *Macroeconomics in the Global Economy*. Englewood Cliffs, N.J.: Prentice Hall.

Samuelson, P. A. & Nordhaus, W. D. (1995). *Economics*. New York: McGraw-Hill Publishing Company.

Slemrod, J. (1996). "On the High-Income Laffer Curve." In *Tax Progressivity and Income Inequality*, J. Slemrod, ed. Cambridge: Cambridge University Press.

Slemrod, J. & Bakija, J. (1996). *Taxing Ourselves: A Citizen's Guide to the Great Debate Over Tax Reform*. Cambridge, MA: MIT Press.

Sokolov, M. (2010)."Fantom teorii nalogooblozhenia (o krivoi' Artura Laffera)" [Phantom of the Taxation Theory (on the Arthur Laffer Curve)].*Ekonomika Ukrainy* [Economy of the Ukraine], No. 7. (In Russian.)

Sokolovskii, L. E. (1989). "Podokhodnyi nalog i ekonomicheskoe povedenie (Vvedenie v literaturu)" [Income Tax and Economic Behavior (Introduction to the Literature)]. *Ekonomika i matematiceskie metody* [Economics and Mathematical Methods], Vol. *25*, No. 4.(In Russian.)

Sokolovskii, L. E. (1992). "Nalog na dobavlennuiu stoimost' i predpriatie, maksimiziriushchee pribil'" [Value-Added Tax and the Profit-Maximizing Enterprise]. *Ekonomika i matematiceskie metody* [Economics and Mathematical Methods], Vol. *28*, No. 4. (In Russian.)

Sowell, T. (2012).*"Trickle Down" Theory and "Tax Cuts for the Rich."* Stanford: Hoover Institution Press.

Steinmo, S. (1993). *Taxation and Democracy.Swedish, British, and American Approaches to Financing the Modern State*. New Haven: Yale University Press.

Stiglitz, J. E. (1988). *Economics of the Public Sector*. New York: W. W. Norton & Company

Stiglitz, J. E. (2003). *The Roaring Nineties*. New York: W. W. Norton & Company.

Thirlwall, A. P. (1969). "Okun's Law and the Natural Rate of Growth." *Southern Economic Journal*, Vol. *36*, No. 1.

Thirlwall, A. P. & Ireland, N. J. (1970). "Okun's Law and the Natural Rate of Growth: Peplay." *Southern Economic Journal*, Vol. *37*, No. 2.

Vishnevskii', V. & Lipnitskii', D. (2000). "Otsenka vozmozhnostei snizhenia nalogovogo bremeni v perekhodnoi ekonomike" [Assessment of the Possibilities for Reducing the Tax Burden in a Transitional Economy]. *Voprosy ekonomiki* [Issues of the Economics], No. 2.

ABOUT THE AUTHORS

Dr. Iuri Ananiashvili is a Professor at Ivane Javakhishvili Tbilisi State University, Head of the Department of Econometrics. He currently teaches econometrics, macroeconomics and macroeconomic modeling at the Faculty of Economics and Business. Dr. Ananiashvili holds a degree of the Candidate of Economic Sciences from the Central Economic-Mathematical Institute of the Academy of Sciences of the USSR (1981, Moscow, Russia), a degree of the Doctor of Economic Sciences from Paata Gugushvili Institute of Economics, the Georgian Academy of Sciences (1998, Tbilisi, Georgia). He is the author of more than 70 articles and four books on the problems of macroeconomics, microeconomics and econometrics. He is also a co-author of two books with Vladimer Papava: Makroekonomikuri regulirebis metodebi da modelebi [Methods and models of macroeconomic regulation] (2003, Tbilisi, Georgia, in Georgian), Nalogi i makroekonomicheskoe ravnovesie: Laffero-keinsianskii' sintez [Taxes and Macroeconomic Equilibrium: Laffer-Keynesian Synthesis] (Stockholm, 2010, in Russian)

Professor Vladimer Papava is a Rector of the Ivane Javakhishvili Tbilisi State University, a Senior Fellow at the Georgian Foundation for Strategic and International Studies and a Chief Research Associate at the Paata Gugushvili Institute of Economics. He was the Minister of Economy of the Republic of Georgia (1994-2000) and a Member of Parliament (2004-2008) (Tbilisi, Republic of Georgia); in 2005-2006 he was a Fulbright Fellow at the Central Asia—Caucasus Institute, The Nitze School—SAIS, Johns Hopkins University (Washington, DC). He is the author more than 300 publications, including works on the theoretical and applied studies post-Communist economies, macroeconomics and economic development. Prof. Papava holds a

Degree of the Candidate of Economic Sciences from Central Economic-Mathematical Institute of the Academy of Sciences of the USSR (1982, Moscow, Russia), a Degree of the Doctor of Economic Sciences from Leningrad State University (1990, Saint-Petersburg, Russia), and Tbilisi State University (1989, Tbilisi, Georgia). His English-language publications include: Financial Globalization and Post-Communist Georgia (New York, 2003) with Vepkhia Chocheli, Splendours and Miseries of the IMF in Post-Communist Georgia (Laredo, TX, 2003), Necroeconomics: The Political Economy of Post-Communist Capitalism (New York, 2005), The Central Caucasus: Problems of Geopolitical Economy (New York, 2008) with Eldar Ismailov, and Economic Reforms in Post-Communist Georgia: Twenty Years After (New York, 2012). He is a co-author of two books with Iuri Ananiashvili: Makroekonomikuri regulirebis metodebi da modelebi [Methods and models of macroeconomic regulation] (2003, Tbilisi, Georgia, in Georgian), Nalogi i makroekonomicheskoe ravnovesie [Taxes and Macroeconomic Equilibrium] (Stockholm, 2010, in Russian).

INDEX

N

O

P

Q

R

U

V

W

Y

Z